Covered in this book:

Ceramics

Types of clay • Tools and equipment • Clay molds, wedging boards and bats • Mixing and pouring plaster • Drying and sizing plaster • Preparing the clay • Methods of forming clay: pinch pot, throwing, etc. • Sculpturing clay • Mold making • Slip casting • Storage and drying • Surface coloring and finishing: underglazes, glazes, overglazes, bisque stains • Decorating • Kilns: types and use

Mosaics

Tools and equipment • Basic materials • Design • Procedures

Stained Glass

Glass cutting • Tools • Grozing • Sanders • The working area: cutting tables and light boxes • Design • Making a pattern • Choosing colors • Cutting patterns for leading and for foiling • Cutting the glass • Copper foil glazing • Traditional lead technique • Setting up a glazing board • Soldering copper fo... ...king • Etching glass • Glass mosaic...

Cover design by Roy Kuhlman

David McKay Company, Inc.
750 Third Avenue
New York, New York 10017

0-679-50762-0

Ceramics, Mosaics,
and Stained Glass

CERAMICS, MOSAICS, and STAINED GLASS

a creative introduction to methods and materials

Edited by Saul Lapidus

A COURIER BOOK

David McKay Company, Inc.
New York

The sections on ceramics and mosaics are adapted from a
U.S. Government Printing Office publication, *Craft Techniques in Occupational Therapy*, Technical Manual 8290. The
adaptation is illustrated by Chris Dec.

Library of Congress Cataloging in Publication Data

Ceramics, mosaics, and stained glass.

    "A Courier book."
    1. Pottery craft. 2. Mosaics. 3. Glass craft.
I. Lapidus, Saul.
TT920.C74   738   77–8008
ISBN 0–679–50762–0 pbk.

10 9 8 7 6 5 4 3 2 1

Book design: ARLENE SCHLEIFER GOLDBERG

CONTENTS

INTRODUCTION

As craft interest strengthens and grows, so does the need for quality instruction. That's what this book is all about. We provide a basic reference manual for three creative crafts. By using detailed text and illustrations, we outline the fundamental techniques used to create useful and/or decorative pieces in the chosen medium.

We believe that if you begin with the easy, then the difficult becomes simpler. Some books "teach" a project and hope you glean the basic skills of the craft as well. But frequently, all that is learned is that particular project. We show you the basic techniques, tools, and procedures of the craft necessary to acquire the general skills needed to go on to any new project. Formal art training is not a prerequisite for understanding a craft, but some knowledge of basic design is, of course, quite helpful. For example, copying or adapting one design to form another is a very useful way to create new ideas. A small object in a large design may often be used as the central theme for a new piece. And keep in mind that when you adopt other designs, you are also creating by combining your personal choices. In a way, all creativity is a new way of using old ideas.

The best way to use this book is to read through each section to gain an overview of the specific craft; then practice the basic skills involved, using some expendable materials. After a short time, cutting, bending, and shaping will come easily and the creative process will proceed on its own. We don't promise that you'll become an expert at any of these crafts—that's up to you. But we can promise to get you involved, and show you the basic elements, techniques, procedures, and tools. We've included glossaries of terms for your convenience. View your tools and equipment as an extension of yourself, and treat them accordingly.

Good luck!

CERAMICS

Ceramics

Ceramics is the general term used to describe the art of making things from clay, which is pliable or plastic in the natural state but becomes hard and durable upon exposure to high temperature. Clay is a simple, formless material with little value until the potter, in processing, shaping, and decorating, changes it into a useful or beautiful object of worth. This art has been going on through the centuries, and even with the inventions of science, working with clay remains a challenge. There is still the suspense of firing a piece in the kiln and awaiting either the pang of disappointment or the thrill of success. Either result serves as a challenge to greater effort.

The field of ceramics includes a wide variety of industrial products such as bricks, tiles, and insulators. Generally, ceramics is confined to such objects as tableware, decorative knick knacks, jewelry, and sculpture. The following terms are pertinent to the field of ceramics.

GLOSSARY

Armature. A form used to support a piece while it is being modeled.

Bat. A slab of plaster or fired clay used to work on or to dry moist clay.

Bisque or biscuit ware. Clay which has been fired without glaze.

Blunging. The process of mixing clay in a blunger, which is a huge mixing machine with rotating paddles.

Bone dry. Clay which is thoroughly air-dried but has not been kiln-fired.

Ceramics. The art of producing clay products.

Clay. Material from which ceramic pieces are formed. The word is generally applied to the material in its natural state before processing.

Coil. A rope-shaped piece of clay.

Crackle. Deliberate crazing of glaze for effect.

Crazing. Minute cracks in the glaze.

Deflocculants. Chemicals (sodium carbonate or sodium silicate) which are added to clay to reduce the amount of water necessary to make it pourable. Used in making slip.

Dry footing. Removing the glaze from the foot, or bottom, of a piece so it can be fired in a kiln without the use of stilts.

Earthenware. Low-fired pottery (under 2,000° F.), usually red or tan in color.

Engobe. A thick layer of slip, usually colored, used for decorating clay.

Fettling. The process of removing the seams from a cast piece.

Glaze. A liquid mash of finely ground minerals applied to the surface of green or bisque ware. After the glaze dries, it is fired in the kiln, giving the piece a glossy, glasslike finish.

Green ware. Clay pieces which have not been fired. Moistening could return this clay to its plastic state.

Grog. Clay which has been fired and ground; used in clay bodies to reduce shrinkage, to give a rough texture, and to prevent warping.

Key. A roll of plastic clay used to hold pieces on the wheel.

Kiln. An oven or furnace used to fire ceramic products.

Kiln wash. A solution of refractory material painted on the floor and shelves of a kiln to keep glaze from sticking.

Kneading. A method of working clay with the fingers or the heel of the hand to obtain a uniform consistency. Also a method of wedging.

Leather hard. Clay which is still moist enough to be carved or burnished easily but is too dry to be plastic.

Modeling wheel or *bench whirler.* A small wheel revolved by hand. Originally used for decorating and banding pottery. Also used in hand building to obtain symmetry.

Mold. A hollow form of pattern usually made of plaster of paris and used for casting or pressing clay into a definite shape.

Overglaze. Colors applied and fired at a low heat after the piece has been glazed.

Plasticity. The capacity to yield to pressure and to hold the form given by that pressure. A quality of clay.

Pyrometric cones. Pyramids made from clay and auxiliary fluxes, used to indicate the heat within the kiln. The composition of the cone determines the melting point.

Rib. A wood base or metal tool used to refine shapes being thrown on a potter's wheel.

Sgraffito. A form of decoration in which the clay body is covered with a coating of contrasting color. The design is cut through the first layer to reveal the body.

Shrinkage. The contraction of a clay piece due to evaporation and expulsion of water during drying and firing.

Sizing. The application of a coating to prevent two pieces, usually of plaster, from sticking together.

Slip. Liquid clay, the consistency of thick cream, used for casting, for slip painting, or for gluing clay parts together.

Slip-casting. The process of pouring slip into a mold, in which it is shaped.

Slurry. Thick slip used frequently to glue two pieces of clay together.

Sprig decoration. Wafer-thin bits of clay formed into decorative shapes to be applied on green ware.

Stacking. Placing shaped pieces in the kiln for firing.

Stilts. Refractory material upon which pottery is placed in the kiln during firing to prevent the flowing glaze from sticking to the kiln furniture.

Template. An outline or pattern used to shape the profile of a piece.

Throwing. Shaping pottery on the wheel.

Turning. Trimming a piece on a lathe or wheel when the clay is leather hard in order to perfect the shape.

Underglaze. Colored decoration applied to green ware or to bisque ware before the glaze is applied.

Warping. Loss of the original shape of a piece as a result of uneven drying and/or firing.

Wedging. Cutting, pounding, slapping, and kneading clay to obtain a uniform texture and to remove all air pockets.

Wedging board. A wood- or plaster-covered surface used for wedging clay.

Wheel. A vertical lathe used by potters for throwing and turning pottery.

CLAY

Clay is a mixture of aluminum, silicon, and chemically combined water which, in most instances, contains various impurities that impart special characteristics. Common clays are kaolin, ball clay, fire clay, stoneware, and common (or red) clay. Most of the ceramic clays used today have been compounded to suit specific requirements and may be purchased in the dry state, in moist form, or as casting slip.

When purchasing clay, more clay per pound is obtained by buying the dry form rather than the moist, as the water is included in the weight of the moist clay. Dry clay must be mixed with water before it is used. To mix clay, use a rustproof container and add the clay to the water rather than the water to the clay. Small amounts can be mixed in a plastic bag (Fig. 1). It is best to allow any clay mixture to stand at least 12 hours before using, as the plasticity of the clay seems to improve with some aging. The clay must then be well wedged. The advantages of using dry clay are that it is less expensive and only the amount that is needed can be mixed, thereby solving the problem of storing moist clay.

Although moist clay is more expensive than dry clay, it is ready to use with little preparation. In some circumstances, this convenience is well worth the cost. To be usable, it must be kept moist in damp boxes or in plastic bags. If it becomes too hard to work easily, a number of thin holes should be poked through the clay to within an inch of the bottom. Water is then poured over the clay and it is left to stand. Finally, it must be mixed, kneaded, and wedged to distribute the water evenly throughout.

Slip is a mixture of clay and water. For casting, chemicals known as deflocculants (sodium silicate and soda ash) are added. With a deflocculant, more clay can be suspended in a given amount of water. Casting slip can be made from dry or moist clay, which is less expensive than purchasing slip by the gallon. The balance of clay, water, and deflocculant is delicate, however, and varies with each type of clay. If this balance is not correct, casting is difficult or impossible. It is sometimes economical to purchase premixed slip to ensure more satisfying and rewarding work. Slip without the deflocculant is used as a mending material to join two pieces of plastic or leather-hard clay; it should be made from the same clay as the piece being mended. Clay is sometimes called slurry when used in this way. Slip is also used for decorating; it

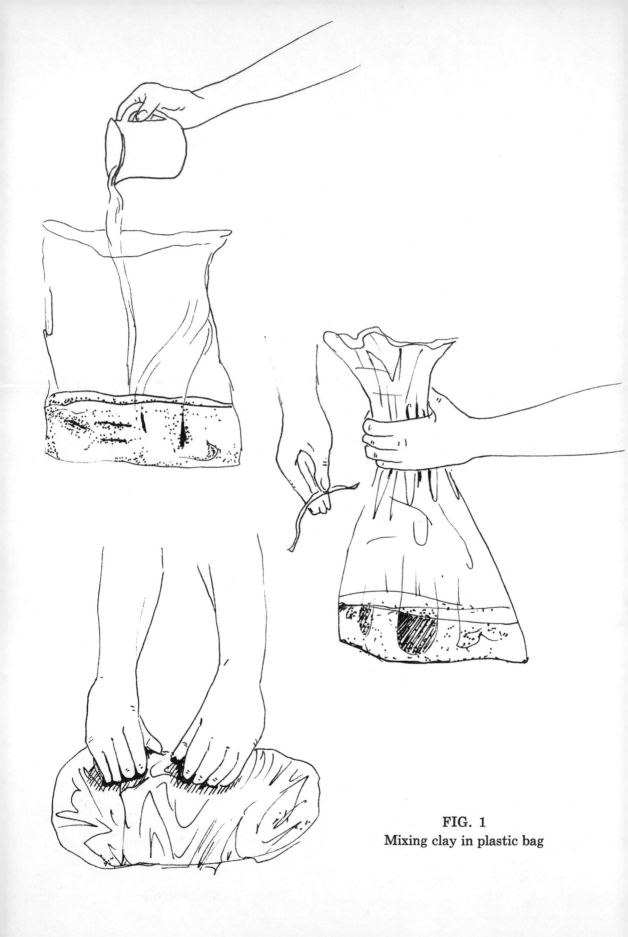

FIG. 1
Mixing clay in plastic bag

may be reconstituted if not fired and should be strained through a fine sieve to remove foreign bodies.

TYPES OF CLAY

Nonfiring clays are those which harden without being baked in a kiln. These clays are suggested for use when no kiln is available.

When no kiln is available, Mexican pottery clay is used because of its self-hardening qualities. This red clay is available in moist form only and can be shaped by any hand method or thrown on the potter's wheel. When dry, the clay is hard and durable but not waterproof. Showcard colors or tempera paints are used for decorating; then a clear protective coating is applied. The coating may be shellac, varnish, or one of the commercial products made especially for this purpose. This is only a protective coating, however, and will not waterproof the piece.

Modeling clay is an oil-based, nontoxic, nonhardening clay available under a number of different trade names. The texture is fine and smooth, and it is commercially available by the pound in pastel or bold, bright colors. It can be modeled or carved, retains fine detail, and is not affected by temperature changes or humidity.

Oven-baked clay is suitable for all modeling techniques. When a piece is completed and dry, it is placed in a regular kitchen oven and baked at 250°–305° F. for 20 minutes, then cooled slowly. The piece will be gray in color. It will also be hard and durable but not waterproof. For decorating, tempera paints or showcard colors and a clear, protective coating are used. This clay comes in moist, ready-to-use form.

Self-hardening clay is a red clay which requires no firing in the kiln. When the piece is completed and air-dried, it becomes strong and durable. Decorating is done with showcard colors or tempera paints, which are covered with a clear protective coating such as shellac, varnish, or one of the commercial products made for this purpose. This clay is available in moist form only.

The most well-known clays for ceramics are the kiln-fired clays. As their name suggests, these must be fired at very high temperatures.

Indian red clay (Cones 06 or 05—1,859° or 1,904° F.) is a favorite with ceramists, perhaps because it is plastic and excellent for all forms of hand modeling. However, it is more likely to shrink and warp than some others. It is a rich red color both before and after firing, which allows for many interesting decorating effects with different glazes and sgraffito designs. The clay is available in dry, moist, and slip form.

Jordan clay (Cones 06 or 2—1,859° or 2,129° F.) is a fine working clay which is a light pink-buff color after it has been fired. It can be used for all kinds of modeling, including throwing, but it is particularly good for slip-casting. It comes in dry and moist forms.

Monmouth clay (Cones 06 or 2—1,859° or 2,129° F.) is one of the smoothest working clays on the market, and it is excellent for all hand-forming methods as well as for throwing. It is available only in moist form and is a medium-buff color after firing.

Porcelain clay (Cones 3 or 6—2,138° or 2,246° F.) requires great firing heat. Before planning to work with it, check to see if the kiln is made to fire porcelain clay to maturity. Also make sure that the glazes will not burn out at these high temperatures. The modeling formula for this clay is recommended for wheel throwing, for sculpture, and for all other methods of hand forming. It has a smooth plastic quality and is light gray before firing, but the bisque is white. This formula is available in both moist and dry form. Porcelain casting slip is made in white, black, pink, peach, blue, aqua, green, and yellow. These colors can be contrasted or combined for interesting decorative effects.

Stoneware (Cones 4 or 8—2,174° or 2,300° F.) also requires great heat. Before planning to work with this clay, check to see if the kiln is made to fire at temperatures high enough to mature stoneware and that the glazes will not burn out at these temperatures. Stoneware is made from natural clays, usually combined to produce a workable plastic clay for modeling and throwing. Because of the chemical makeup and the high firing temperature, the bisque will hold water if it is fired to full maturity. Since the bisque is waterproof and attractive in color, unique effects can be obtained with partial glazing, slip-trailing, and underglaze decoration. This clay is available in dry and moist forms.

Terra cotta (Cones 06 or 5—1,859° or 2,201° F.) is best suited for rough-textured and outdoor pieces such as tiles, planters, and lamps. This clay is a combination of red and buff clays mixed with more grog than other clays contain. As a result, there is little cracking, shrinking, or warping, and it lends itself well to the forming of large pieces.

White talc (Cones 06 or 05—1,859° or 1,904° F.) is very versatile and can be used for hand forming, throwing, and slip-casting. It is gray-white before it is fired, but the bisque is intensely white. Decorating colors and transparent glazes retain their true color and brilliance on this bisque, a quality desired by many ceramists. It is available in dry and moist forms as well as in slip.

CERAMIC TOOLS AND EQUIPMENT

Bamboo brushes (Fig. 2) are used to apply underglaze.

Calipers (wooden) (Fig. 3) are used to measure outside diameters when turning a piece on a potter's wheel.

The clay pull (Fig. 4) is used to cut finished projects from the potter's wheel and to cut clay.

The fettling knife (Fig. 5) is used for cleaning green ware, removing mold marks, trimming, and general smoothing.

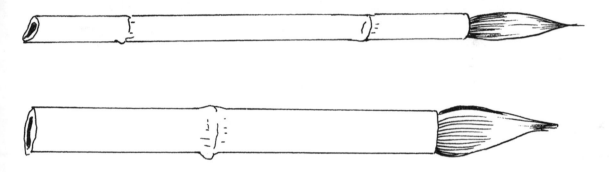

FIG. 2
Bamboo brushes

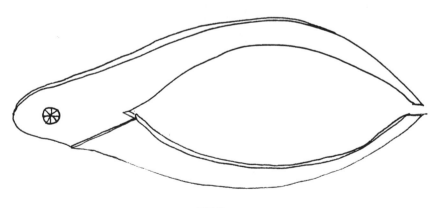

FIG. 3
Calipers

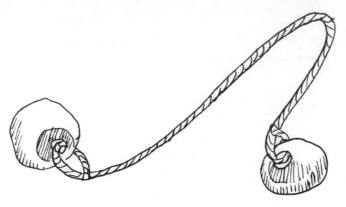

FIG. 4
Clay pull

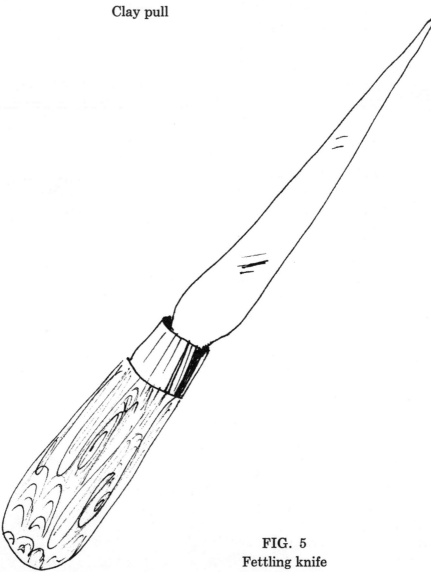

FIG. 5
Fettling knife

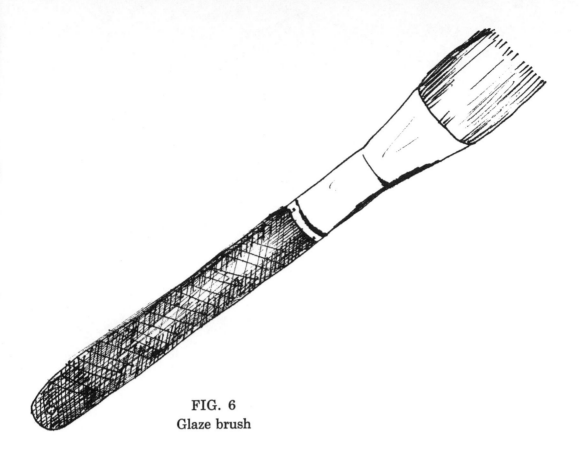

FIG. 6
Glaze brush

The glaze brush (Fig. 6) is a soft-hair brush, usually camel's hair, approximately ¾" to 1" wide, used for applying glaze.

Metal lifters (Fig. 7) are used as an aid in lifting projects from the potter's wheel.

Modeling tools (Fig. 8) are used for shaping or modeling clay objects.

Needlepoint or lace tools (Fig. 9) are used for trimming and cross-hatching with various techniques of construction such as slab or throwing.

Sgraffito and cleanup tools (Fig. 10) are used to incise a design in green ware, to smooth rough spots, or to trim seams left by molds.

The elephant-ear sponge is a fine-grain sponge (Fig. 11) used to smooth green ware, remove excess water, and moisten leather-hard clay projects before glazing.

The slip tracer or trailer is a tool (Fig. 12) used for decorating. It is filled with slip and slowly squeezed to expel slip, thereby leaving a trail or decoration.

Throwing ribs (wooden) (Fig. 13) are an aid used in shaping and raising a cylinder on the potter's wheel.

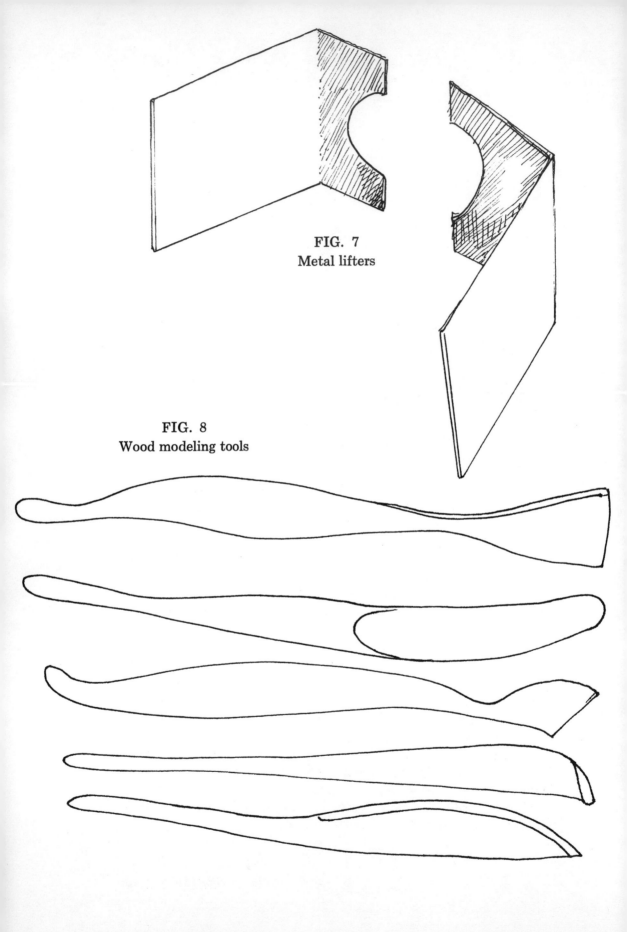

FIG. 7
Metal lifters

FIG. 8
Wood modeling tools

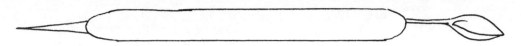

FIG. 9
Needlepoint or lace tool

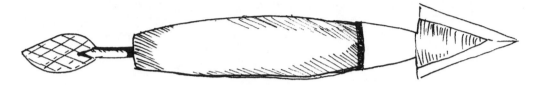

FIG. 10
Sgraffito and cleanup tool

FIG. 11
Elephant ear sponge

Double-wire end or loop tools (Fig. 14) are used to remove excess clay in modeling, throwing, and sculpture.

The rolling pin (Fig. 15) is used to flatten clay for the slab method of construction.

A bat (Fig. 16) is a flat slab of plaster or bisque used for modeling or throwing clay. It is also used to dry out clay.

A damp box (Fig. 17) is a storage area with extremely high humidity, designed to keep clay from drying out. It must have a rustproof lining and a tight-fitting door and be equipped with open shelves to allow for circulation of moisture throughout the box. It is usually available where ceramics are sold, or it can be hand-made—an old icebox is ideal. A large plaster slab at the bottom of the box may be kept water-soaked to maintain the humidity in the box.

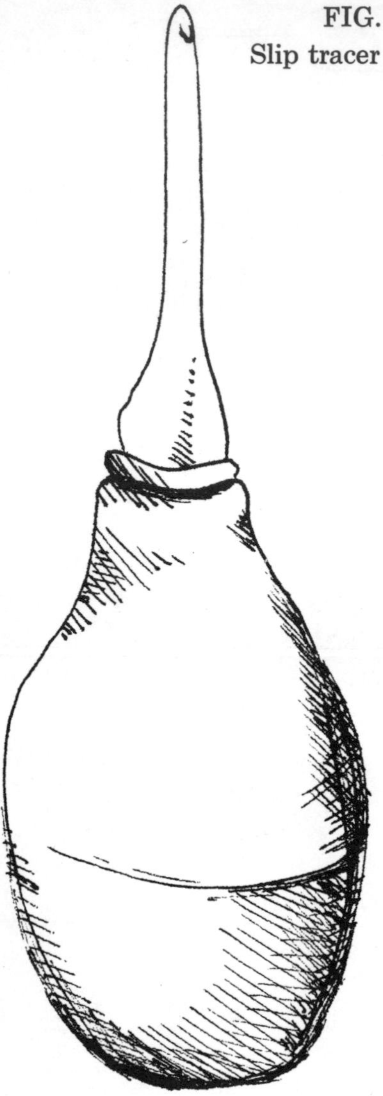

FIG. 12
Slip tracer or trailer

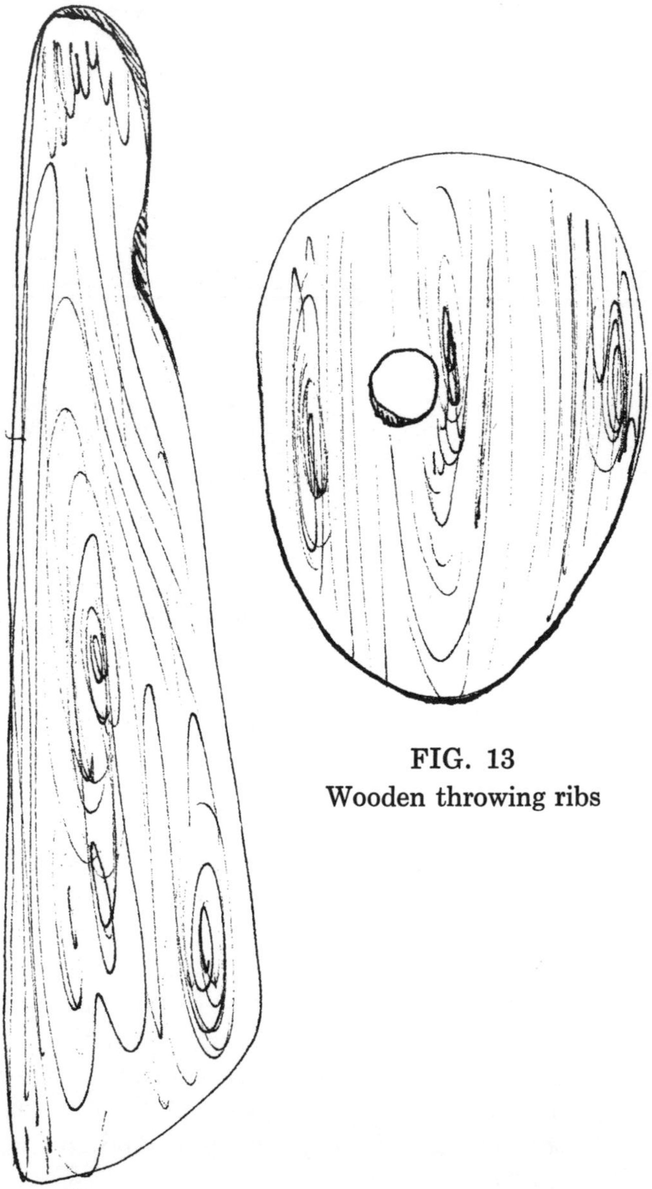

FIG. 13
Wooden throwing ribs

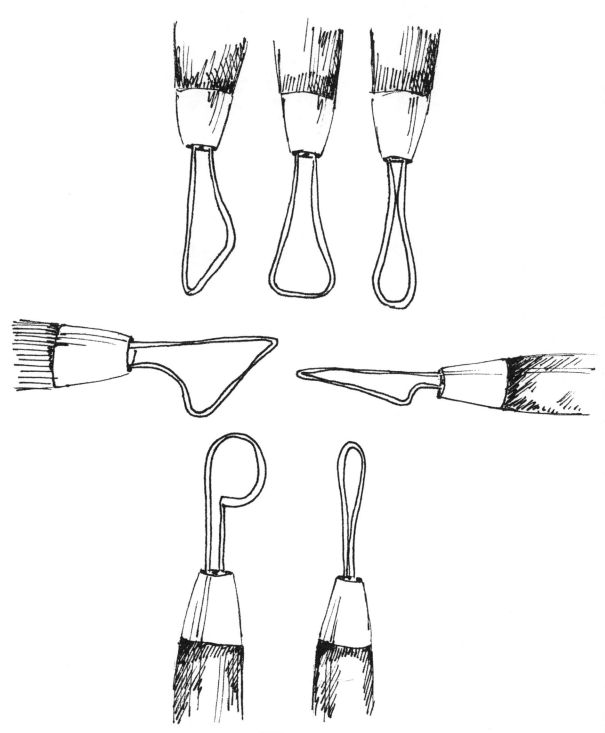

FIG. 14
Double-wire end or loop tools

FIG. 15

Wooden rolling pin

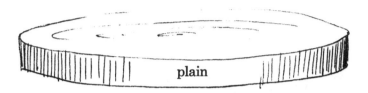

plain

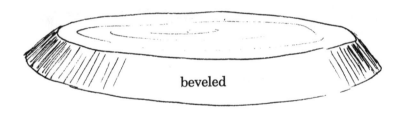

beveled

FIG. 16

Plaster bats

The decorating wheel (Fig. 18) usually has an 8″ wheel head marked with concentric circles. It rotates on ball bearings and is used for modeling, sculpturing, banding, spraying, and decorating. When the wheel is transported, it must be picked up by the base or the wheel will come off.

Safety goggles are used to protect the eyes when grinding and spraying ceramic glaze.

The grinder (Fig. 19) is clamped to the table or workbench and has a fine carborundum wheel attached. This hand-operated tool is used to remove irregularities from the foot of bisque ware and dripping or stilt marks from glazed ware.

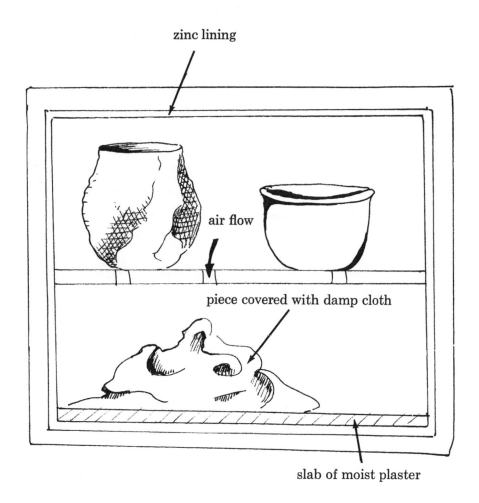

zinc lining

air flow

piece covered with damp cloth

slab of moist plaster

FIG. 17

Cross section of clamp box

Electric kilns can be top-loading (Fig. 20A) or side-loading (Fig. 20B). These ovens are designed to reach the high temperatures necessary to fire clay to its maturity.

The mortar and pestle (Fig. 21) are used for mixing and grinding glazes.

A pitcher (Fig. 22) is used to pour strained slip into molds.

A pyrometer (Fig. 23) installed on a kiln indicates firing chamber temperatures. This is an electronic and mechanical device and should be used in conjunction with a pyrometric cone for safe, sure firings.

The spray gun contains the glaze or englobes to be applied, and

FIG. 18
Decorating wheel

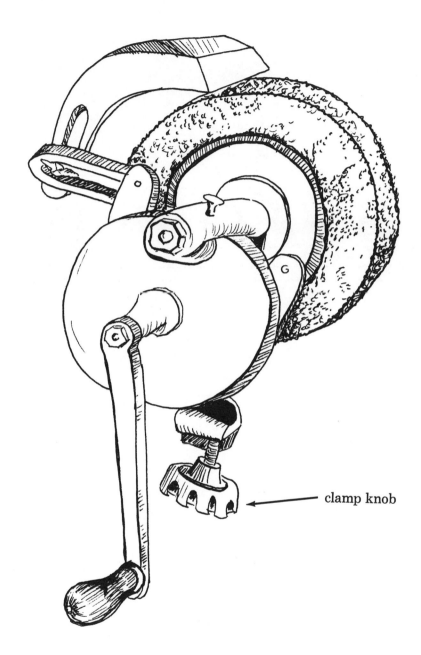

clamp knob

FIG. 19
Clamp knob hand grinder

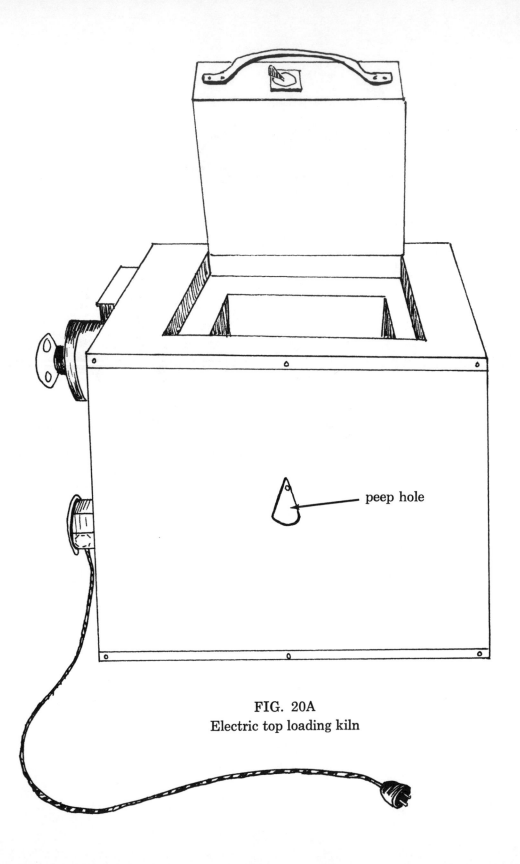

peep hole

FIG. 20A
Electric top loading kiln

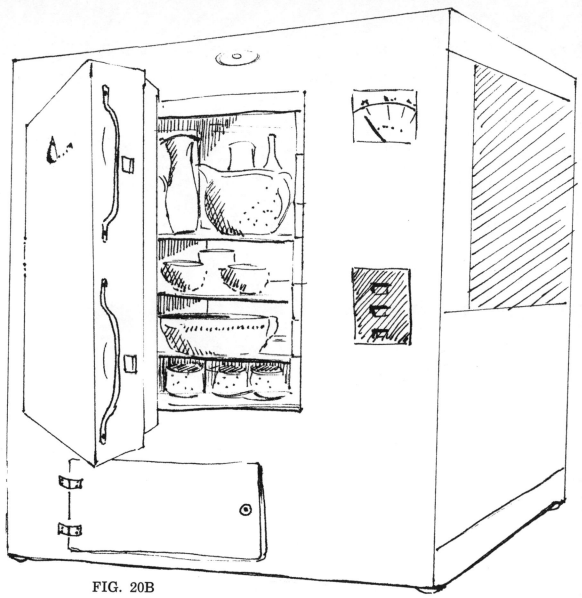

FIG. 20B
Electric side loading kiln

the compressor (Fig. 24) provides the proper supply of air to spray. A 45-pound air pressure is recommended. The compressor should be equipped with a safety valve to prevent pressure buildup from going too high.

The spray booth is equipped with an electric exhaust fan (Fig. 25) that pulls glaze dust into a fireproof impregnated filter located in front of the fan at the back of the booth or box. A decorating wheel is generally used to hold the ware as it is being sprayed, so that it may be rotated for an even coating of glaze.

FIG. 21
Mortar and pestle

FIG. 22
Atcher

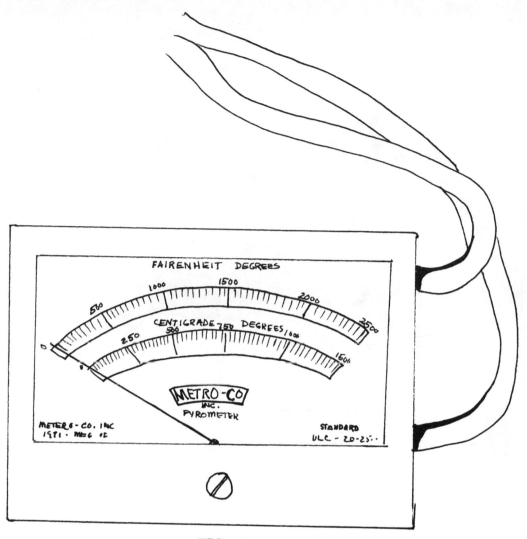

FIG. 23
Pyrometer

Potter's wheels can be foot powered, also called kick wheel (Fig. 26A), or electric powered (Fig. 26B). Some electric wheels have a two-speed control; others have a rheostat for variable speeds. All are used for turning cylindrical shapes of ceramic materials.

A protective spray mask (Fig. 27) is used to prevent inhalation of glass or glaze during spraying procedures.

Kiln shelves are thin but strong shelves (Fig. 28) with crescent-shaped notches to facilitate quick heat diffusion. They are made of silicon carbide, a refractory material. These shelves are placed in a firing chamber, and ceramic ware is stacked on them. The top of each kiln shelf must be coated with kiln wash.

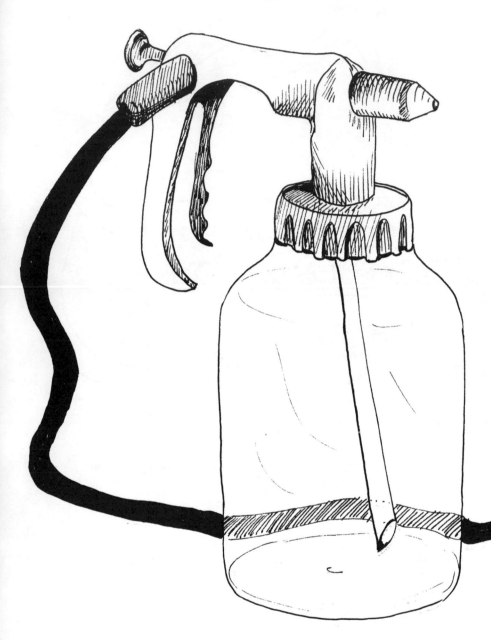

FIG. 24
Spray gun

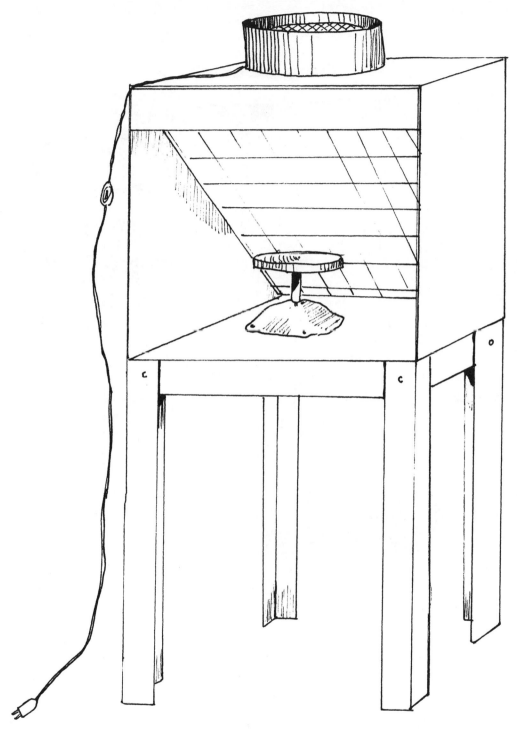

FIG. 25
Spray booth with exhaust fan

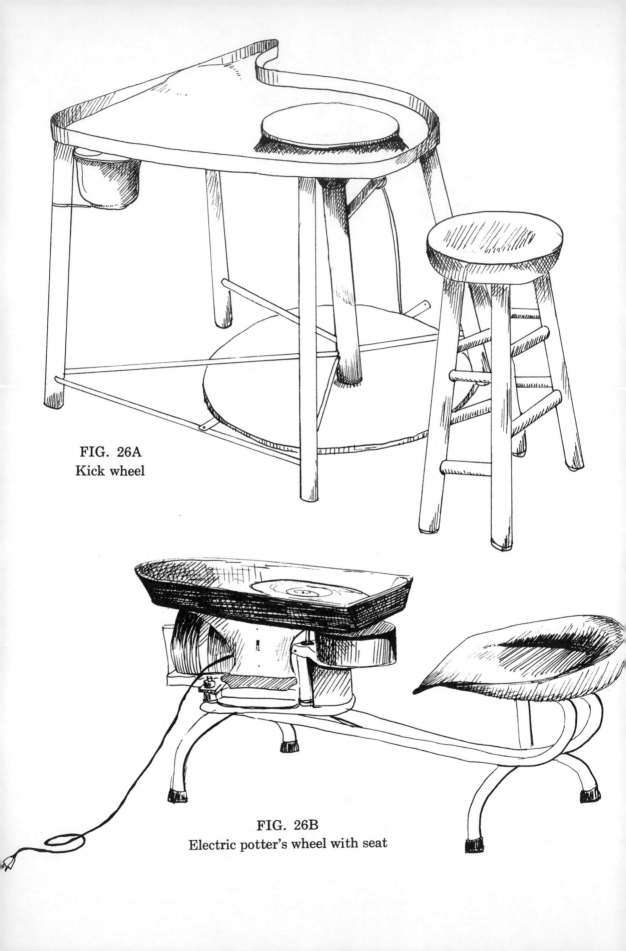

FIG. 26A
Kick wheel

FIG. 26B
Electric potter's wheel with seat

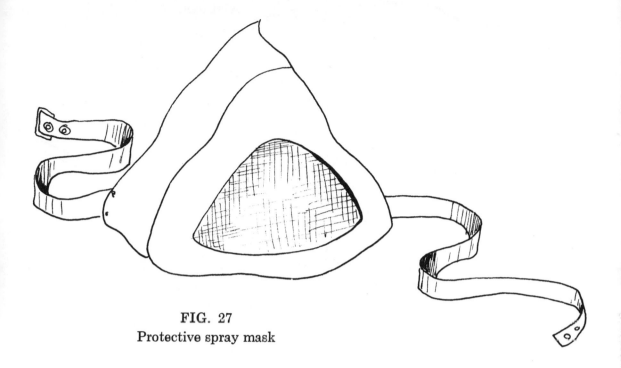

FIG. 27
Protective spray mask

Shelf supports (Fig. 28A) are used in the firing chamber of a kiln to prop, support, or space kiln shelves when stacking ceramic ware in the kiln.

Clay is wedged on a wedging board (Fig. 29). If the clay is too moist, wedging is done on the plaster part; if the moisture content is right, it is done on the wooden part. The wooden areas of a wedging board are covered with a water-resistant lacquer. The fine steel wire, which is for cutting clay, is held taut by a turnbuckle, and the absorbent plaster section should be smooth.

CLAY MOLDS, WEDGING BOARDS, AND BATS

Molds, wedging boards, and bats for sculpturing and throwing are made from plaster of paris. Because of this extensive use, one of the first things a ceramist must learn is to mix and to form plaster. Plaster of paris is a gypsum rock that has been specially heated to remove its moisture. The heating process reduces the rock to a soft material which is easily crushed into a white powder. This powder has an affinity for water; when it is mixed with water, it sets or crystallizes once more into a hard, white solid state.

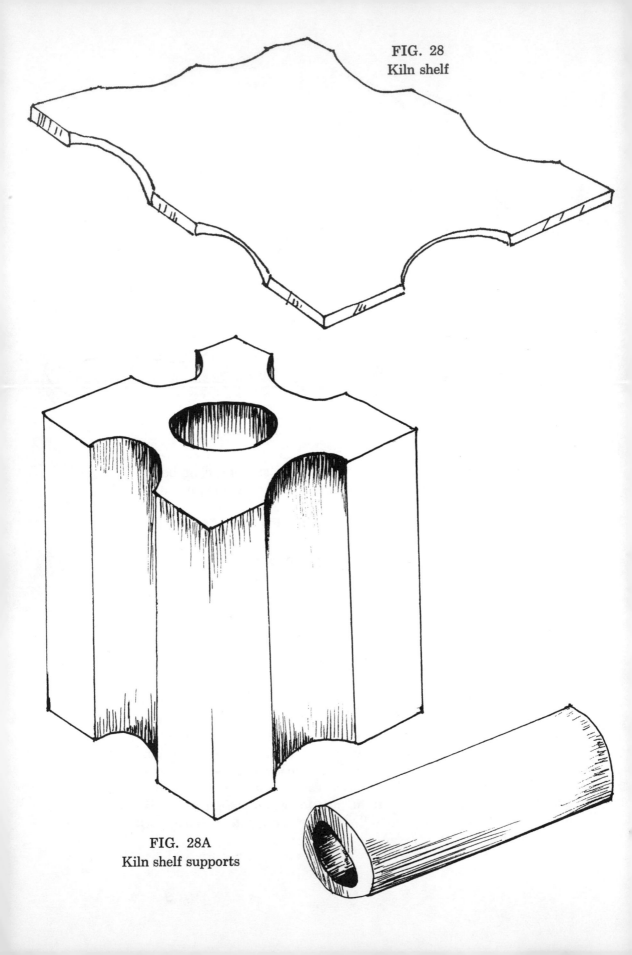

FIG. 28
Kiln shelf

FIG. 28A
Kiln shelf supports

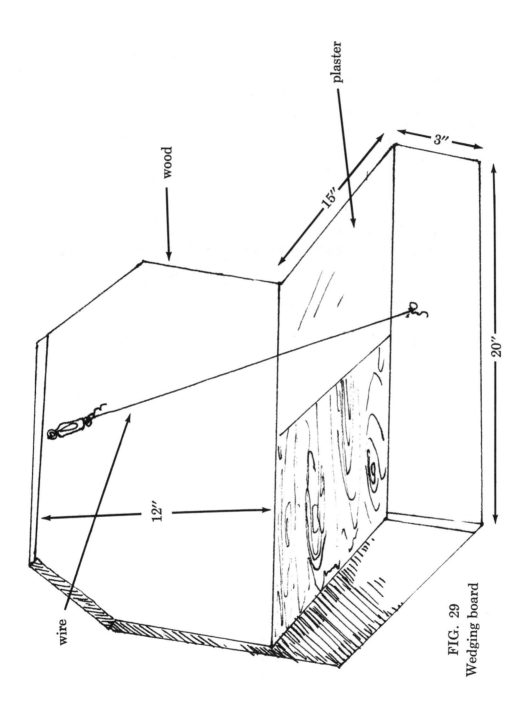

FIG. 29
Wedging board

MIXING AND POURING PLASTER

When mixing plaster, both water and plaster must be measured accurately. The correct proportion for making molds is 2¾ pounds of plaster to 1 quart of water. A greater proportion of plaster produces a mix which is too hard or dense and not sufficiently absorbent for molds. A lesser proportion produces a weak substance which crumbles easily. In mixing, the water is measured first and put in a pail or bowl; then the plaster is weighed and sprinkled into the water. (If the plaster is sprinkled into the water rather than being poured in, there is less likelihood of it lumping.) When all of the plaster has been sprinkled in, the mixture should be allowed to slake, or set, for 2 minutes. This slaking period is important, for if the plaster is stirred too soon, it will form lumps. After slaking, stirring should be done by hand in such a way that the whole mass is agitated and the air bubbles are drawn out. If a pail or deep bowl is used, a good method of stirring is to put the hand—palm upward—on the bottom of the pail and wiggle the fingers vigorously so that the plaster is forced up to the top (Fig. 30). In a small container, the mixture should be stirred so that the fingers rub the bottom of the container. Stirring should continue for 2 to 3 minutes after the plaster is mixed, or until the plaster begins to thicken.

The plaster is ready to pour when the mixture is thick enough so that a finger drawn over the surface leaves a slight trace. Shortly after this, it begins to set. Plaster must be poured slowly, steadily, and smoothly without any splashing, so that no air bubbles are trapped and no vacant spaces are formed. It is good to work on a table which can be jarred or vibrated right after the plaster has been poured so that air bubbles can be forced to the surface.

PLASTER BATS

Round plaster bats are used extensively in ceramics as movable platforms for modeling and throwing or as a place to put wet clay for drying. To make one, a pie tin about 6″ to 8″ in diameter can be used. Oil or vaseline is rubbed on the pan, but all excess is wiped off before the plaster is poured. More than enough plaster should be poured in the pan and, as it begins to set, it should be jarred to release any air bubbles; a straightedge or ruler should be drawn

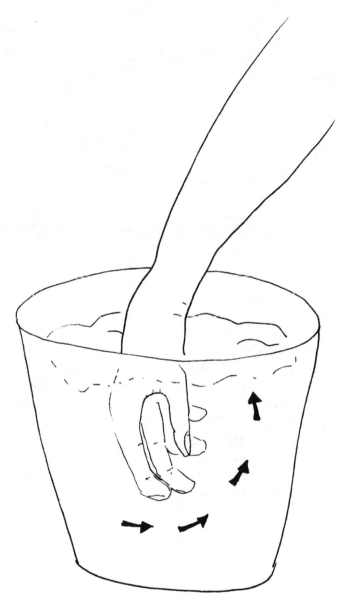

FIG. 30
Stirring plaster

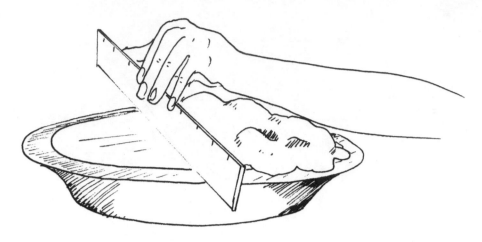

FIG. 31

Leveling the top of a plaster bat

across the top to level it (Fig. 31); then it must be jiggled a bit to get the surface smooth again.

Removable plaster bats are frequently used on the potter's wheel as a base for throwing. It is possible to purchase a special throwing headset (Fig. 32), which also serves as a mold for making bats. This head consists of a recessed aluminum wheel head, which replaces the regular head on the wheel, and an aluminum mold for casting plaster bats. When a piece is thrown on a bat in the recessed head, both the piece and the bat may be removed and set aside for drying without having to remove the piece from the bat. Another bat can be placed in the recess, and the wheel is ready for use again immediately.

DRYING PLASTER

Freshly made plaster feels warm and moist as it sets or becomes firm. As it begins to dry, it feels cool and damp. This coolness is present until the plaster is completely dry. To test for dryness, the plaster is held to the cheek. When it no longer feels cool, it is dry. Drying may take from 2 to 6 days, depending upon the thickness of the piece and the atmospheric conditions. To hasten the drying process, the plaster can be placed near a *warm* radiator, but not on it, or the plaster will get too hot and weaken and crumble.

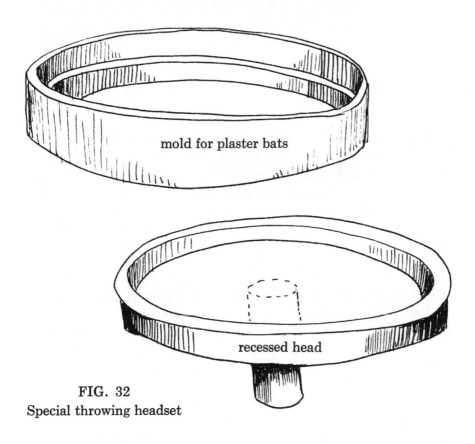

mold for plaster bats

recessed head

FIG. 32
Special throwing headset

SIZING PLASTER

Plaster may be poured onto moist clay or a clean sheet of glass; when it hardens, it will separate from the other material without sticking. If it is poured onto another piece of plaster, however, it will stick. To prevent sticking, soap sizing is used. An easy way of preparing sizing is to put a cake of soap in the bottom of a gallon jar, fill the jar with hot water, cover it and shake vigorously, then let it stand overnight. The next day there will be a thick layer at the bottom of the jar and a clear liquid at the top. The clear liquid at the top is used for the sizing. When all the clear liquid has been used, hot water is again added to the layer at the bottom; it is then shaken vigorously and left to stand overnight. Sizing must be applied to the plaster in several successive applications, each of which is thoroughly wiped off after application. The first application should be very thin so it will soak into the plaster. Sizing may be applied with a soft brush and wiped off with a sponge, or a sponge may be used for both operations.

PREPARING THE CLAY

Clay must be well wedged and pliable before a project is started. Wedging removes the air bubbles that can cause a piece to explode in the kiln, and it gives the clay an even texture throughout. While wedging, it is also possible to alter the moisture content. To wedge a lump of clay, hold it in both hands and push it through the wire on the wedging board so that it is cut in two. On the cut surface there will probably be air spaces (Fig. 33A). To force the air out of the clay, *throw* one of the two pieces of clay onto the surface of the wedging board, *cut part away*, then throw the other piece of clay on the first piece in the same manner. The two pieces will land one on top of the other and form one lump of clay. Pick up this lump and again cut it in two on the wire and throw the two pieces on the board, one on top of the other as before. Repeat these steps 20 to 25 times, then check to see if all air bubbles are out of the clay (Fig. 33B). If they are not, continue wedging until the clay is *entirely* free of air. The dry plaster half of the board will absorb some of the moisture from the clay. This can be prevented by tacking canvas over the plaster or over the wooden half of the board and wedging on the canvas. More moisture can be added to the clay by poking holes and adding water, then kneading the clay and wedging it.

METHODS OF FORMING CLAY

There are innumerable methods of forming clay, both in the commercial field and in hand methods. Those methods most practical for use are the following.

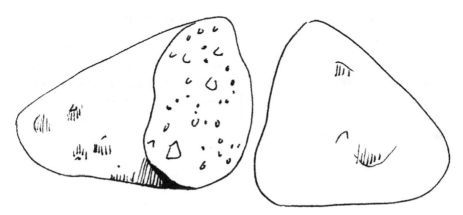

FIG. 33A
Poorly wedged (air bubbles)

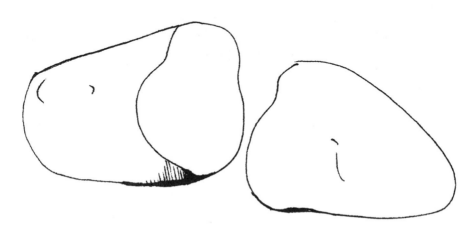

FIG. 33B
Wedged (no air bubbles)

PINCH POT

This is one of the most simple methods of forming clay. Frequently the beginner is asked to start with a pinch-pot piece to get the "feel" of the clay, to know how it responds and what it will do. The hands are the only tools used to form the clay in the pinch-pot method.

(1) Take a piece of wedged clay approximately the size of an orange.

(2) Press the thumb into the center of the ball to within about ½" from the bottom.

(3) Keep one hand cupped around the ball and rotate it as the thumb of the other hand presses the sides into an even wall about ½" thick (Fig. 34). If the clay begins to crack or pull apart, it is too dry. Add a little moisture by dipping the fingers in water, and then continue the forming motions.

(4) When the wall is even, smooth the top or open edges and flatten the bottom so it will set evenly. Then put the piece aside to dry.

COIL METHOD

In this method, coils of clay (Fig. 35) are made, then joined together in a special way so as to form a piece.

(1) Roll the wedged clay on a flat surface. This is done by taking a ball of clay about the size of a golf ball and rolling it with the palms of the hands back and forth on a flat surface until it is a smooth, round coil. Start to roll the coil in the center and roll toward the ends. There should be no cracks in the coil, as cracks will trap air and cause the piece to explode when fired. If the coil cracks when it is bent, the clay is too dry, so water must be added. Coils should usually range from ⅜" in diameter for small articles to 1" in diameter for large pieces. The coils should be used as soon as they are made or they should be covered with plastic, because they dry quickly if left in the open.

(2) As a guide in shaping the object to be formed, make a profile drawing and from it cut a cardboard template. This method is used for the more complex shapes, but for simple forms like cylinders and ovals, the template is not necessary. If a certain size

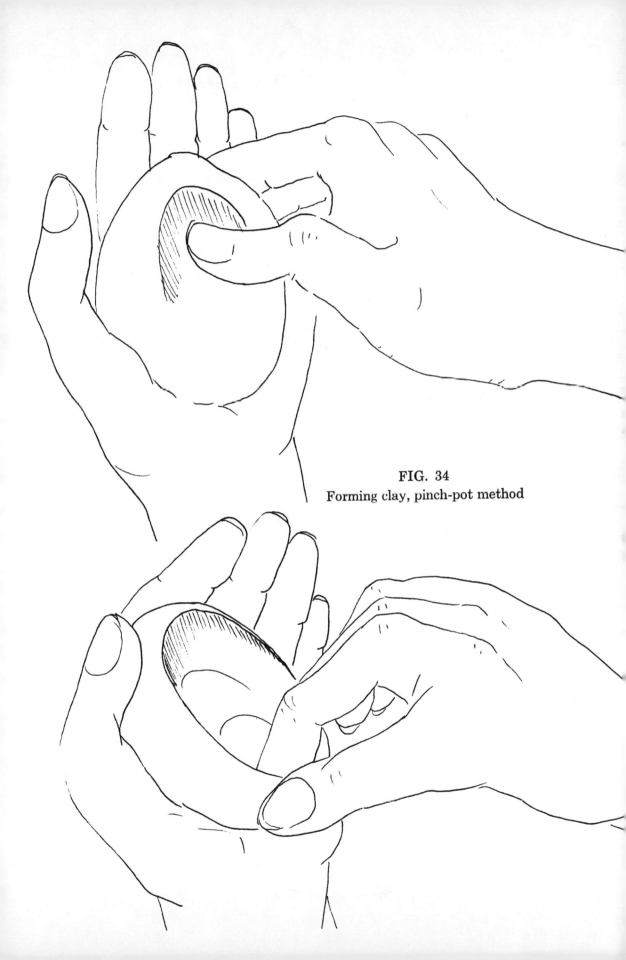

FIG. 34
Forming clay, pinch-pot method

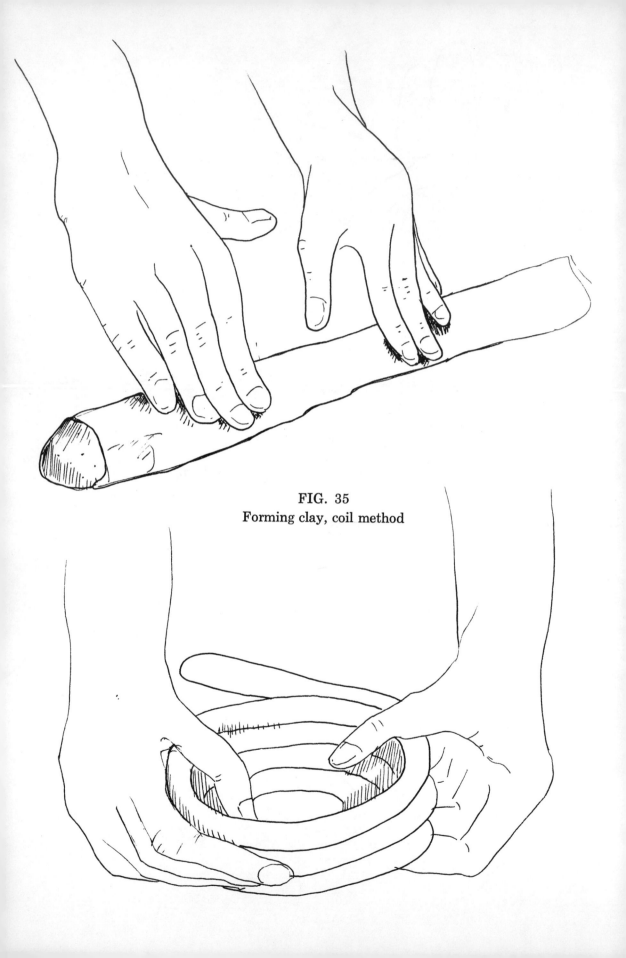

FIG. 35
Forming clay, coil method

piece is desired, the template should be made one-tenth larger than the finished product to allow for the loss in size due to shrinkage of clay.

(3) Prepare the base of the piece by rolling a ball of clay with a rolling pin between two ½″ wooden strips. Cut the desired shape of the base from this ½″-thick slab of clay and place it on a plaster bat. Rough up the top edge of the base where the coil is to be placed with a tool or the edge of a piece of screening; then coat the rough area with slip. Treat the first coil similarly and apply it to the base. Move the two pieces of clay back and forth, and then press them firmly together. Continue to add coils in this manner, placing one on top of the other. When the article is about half completed, stop and smooth all joints, both inside and out. Then apply more coils until the proper height and shape are attained. The walls can then be smoothed until they are of uniform thickness. If a template is used, refer to it frequently to maintain the proper contour. Apply the last coil to the top, and taper or bevel the end of the coil to form a smooth ending. Finish off by smoothing with a damp sponge.

CLAY HUMP MOLD

(1) Make a mold by shaping a high hump of moist clay. All sides of the hump should slope toward the top, with no undercuts. Cover the hump with several layers of moist cheesecloth.

(2) Place a fresh clay slab ¼″, ⅜″, or ½″ thick over the mold and shape to form with the hand. Smooth the clay slab with a wet sponge and flexible scraper.

(3) Trim around the edge of the clay with a fettling knife, and smooth the edges with a sponge.

(4) When the piece is dry enough to retain its shape (leather hard), remove it from the mold. Smooth the edges with a sponge and flatten the bottom with a metal scraper, or add clay legs to keep it from rocking.

HAMMOCK METHOD

(1) Stretch a damp cloth loosely across an empty box.

(2) Make a depression in the cloth to the shape desired and

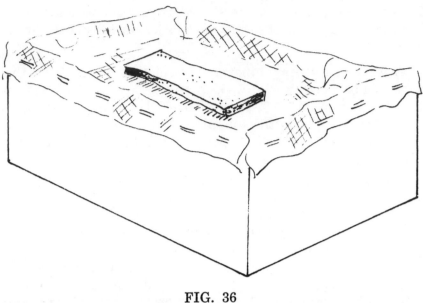

FIG. 36
Hammock method

thumbtack or staple the cloth around the edge of the box to hold it in place. Make sure there are no folds in the cloth, as they will mark the finished piece.

(3) Roll a slab of clay to the desired thickness and place it in the hammock (Fig. 36).

(4) Readjust the shape of the hammock, if necessary, by adjusting the tension of the cloth.

(5) Be sure the piece is deep enough. Pieces that are too shallow tend to flatten out during the bisque firing. To prevent this, prop areas that would possibly flatten with stilts or with balls of clay in the bisque firing.

SLAB METHOD

(1) Knead and wedge a ball of clay the approximate size needed and roll it out into a slab (Fig. 37), using a pair of sticks. One stick is put on each side of the clay to hold the rolling pin up so the clay will be the desired thickness. The sticks may be ¼", ⅜", ½", or ¾" thick, depending upon the thickness needed for the piece to be made. Because clay shrinks, the wet clay must be thicker than is desired for the finished product.

(2) Cut a pattern from paper to the chosen shape, allowing for the thickness of the clay. Lay the pattern on the clay slab (Fig. 38) and cut around it with a fettling knife.

(3) Assemble the cut sections on a canvas or smooth plywood surface. Clay slip is used as an adhesive to join the slabs. Rough the surface to be joined with a sharp pointed tool, apply slip, and put the pieces together. Settle the pieces in with a little back-and-forth motion; then press them together.

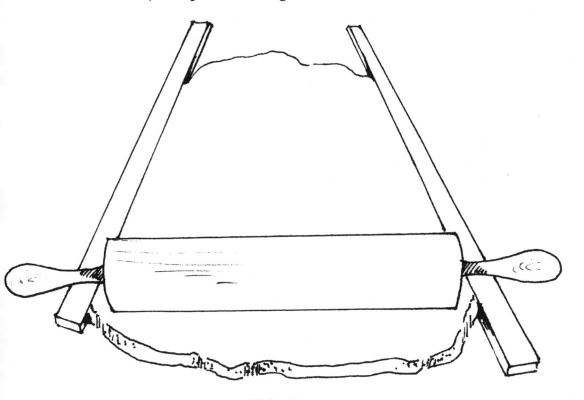

FIG. 37
Making a clay slab

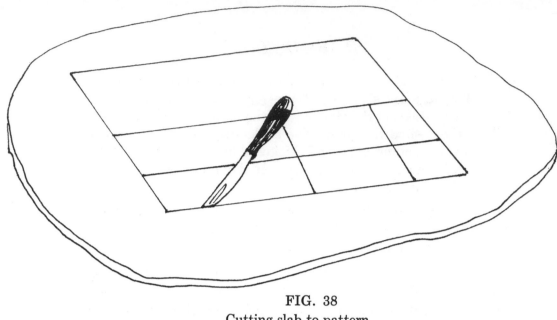

FIG. 38
Cutting slab to pattern

(4) To strengthen the joints, press ⅛″ coils of clay along the edges and corners (Fig. 39), use a wooden stick to press the coils into the corners, and smooth them with a finger dipped in water.

THROWING

Throwing on the potter's wheel is considered by many to be the most interesting and satisfying method of forming clay. It requires patience and practice, but the rewards are well worth the effort. Each ceramist develops the methods that suit him best. As a result, there are nearly as many throwing techniques as there are ceramists who throw. The steps and suggestions given herein are fundamental principles from which the student's own skill and methods may be developed.

Because the head of the wheel turns counterclockwise, place the right hand on the outside of the form and the left hand on the inside. In this way, the clay is turning away from the fingertips, making them less likely to dig in and puncture or pull the piece being shaped.

One of the most important things to note throughout the entire throwing process is that the hands are usually used as a unit, with one braced against the other. If this is not done, the pressure on the piece easily becomes uneven, throwing it off center. This prac-

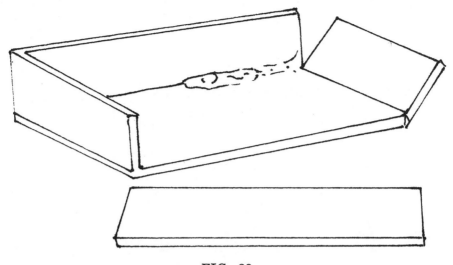

FIG. 39
Strengthening the joints

tice is very important for the beginner to follow as he is developing skill and becoming acquainted with the clay.

Always keep the hands wet while throwing. If they become too dry, the clay will be pulled off center.

Keep water out of the base of the piece being thrown. If this is not done, it will absorb into the piece, which will then lose strength. To get the water out of the base, use a damp elephant-ear sponge.

The condition of the clay is important to good throwing. If the clay is sticky to touch, it is too moist and wedging should be done on dry plaster. If cracks appear when the finger is pressed into the clay ball, it is too dry and water must be added during wedging. The clay must be completely wedged for throwing—air pockets in the clay can throw the piece off center. After the clay is thoroughly wedged, it is formed into a round ball. The amount of clay in the ball determines the size of the thrown piece. A piece the size of a large orange is a good starting size.

If the piece is to be thrown directly on the wheel head, be sure the metal is dry. If a bat is used, put it in place on the wheel head and dampen it a little. A pan of water and a sponge are kept within easy reach while throwing.

The steps below should be followed in making a simple piece. They must be mastered before more elaborate throwing can be accomplished.

FIG. 40
Tossing the clay

(1) Start the wheel moving and toss the ball of clay onto the wheel as near the center as possible (Fig. 40).

(2) Center, or master, the clay. Dip the hands in water, then stabilize the upper arms by pressing them firmly against the rib cage. With the wheel turning rapidly, hold the hands firmly against the clay with the thumbs riding on top, and force the clay ball into the shape of a cone (Fig. 41). Then, force the clay down again by gently pushing the top of the cone (Fig. 42). Repeat this several times to center the clay on the wheel and condition the clay. As this is done, the clay and hands may become too dry and cause a dragging. When this happens, dip the hands in water again.

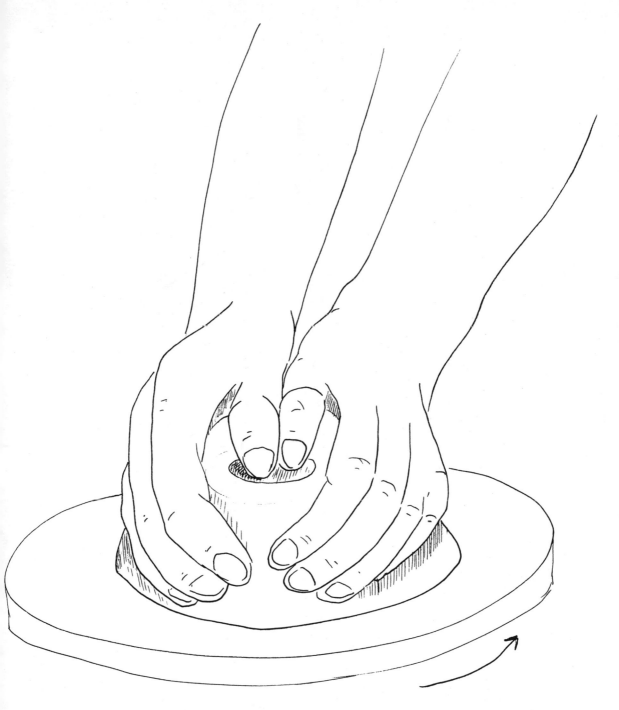

FIG. 41
Centering the clay

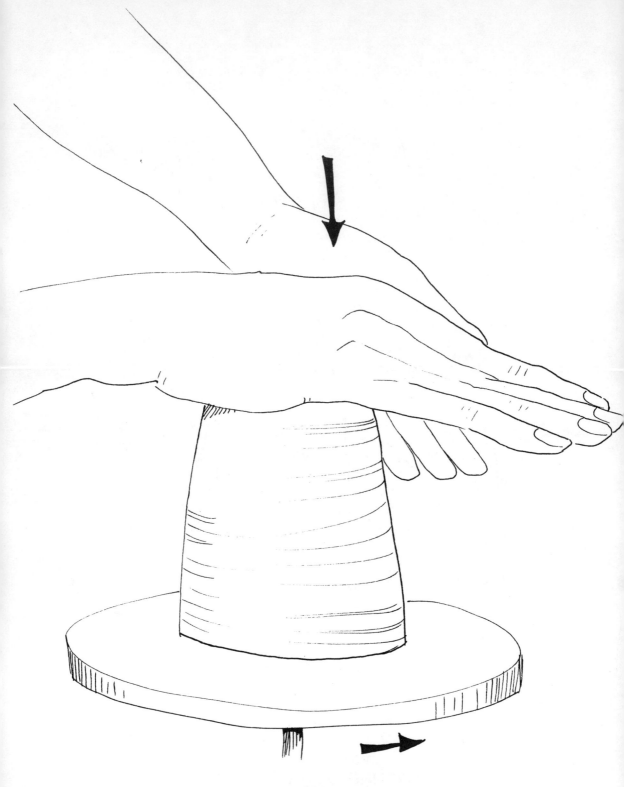

FIG. 42
Pushing the clay down

(3) Open the clay. With the arms still braced and with fast speed on the wheel, hold the hands against the side of the clay with thumbs braced (Fig. 43). Gradually push the tips of the thumbs down in the center of the clay to make an impression in the top. When the depression has been made to within about ½″ of the bat, keep the left hand in place against the outside of the clay and move the right hand over to enlarge the opening made by the thumbs.

(4) Raise the cylinder. Press the knuckle of the right index finger against the outside of the clay and press the left index finger outward against the inside of the clay wall. Keep the thumb of the left hand braced against the back of the right hand. Start at the bottom of the cylinder, then slowly and evenly bring the two hands straight up together, pulling the clay into a cylinder (Figs. 44 and 45). A beginner may not be able to raise the cylinder completely at one time, so the raising step may have to be repeated until the cylinder is tall enough.

(5) To make the cylinder taller and narrower, hold the heels of the hands together and, with the fingers, squeeze in evenly around the cylinder, constricting it to the more narrow shape (Fig. 46). This is called choking. Squeezing too hard or too rapidly when choking will make the cylinder twist. After the cylinder is choked, the raising process can be repeated to make a taller cylinder with a thinner wall. Of course, the cylinder must be left wide enough to accommodate the left hand.

(6) Shaping is making bulges and indentations in the cylinder. Have the fingers of the left hand pressing the cylinder out from the inside and the right hand supporting the clay from the outside, or the right hand pressing the cylinder in to make it smaller in places. While shaping, lock the thumbs for support (Fig. 47).

(7) Skilled ceramists can make a piece with an even top edge, but beginners' work often comes out with an uneven rim. If this happens, cut the uneven edge from the piece while the wheel is turning. Hold a knife or a needlepoint tool against the outside of the cone where the cut is to be made, and gently push it toward the fingers of the left hand, which are held inside the cone at the top (Fig. 48). As soon as the cut is complete, flip the cut ring off the piece as it is held on the knife and the fingers. After the top is cut, smooth it with the fingers and then carefully with a sponge.

(8) Remove any excess water collected in the bottom of the cone from time to time with a damp sponge. If it is allowed to stand, it will soak into the clay and weaken the bottom of the piece.

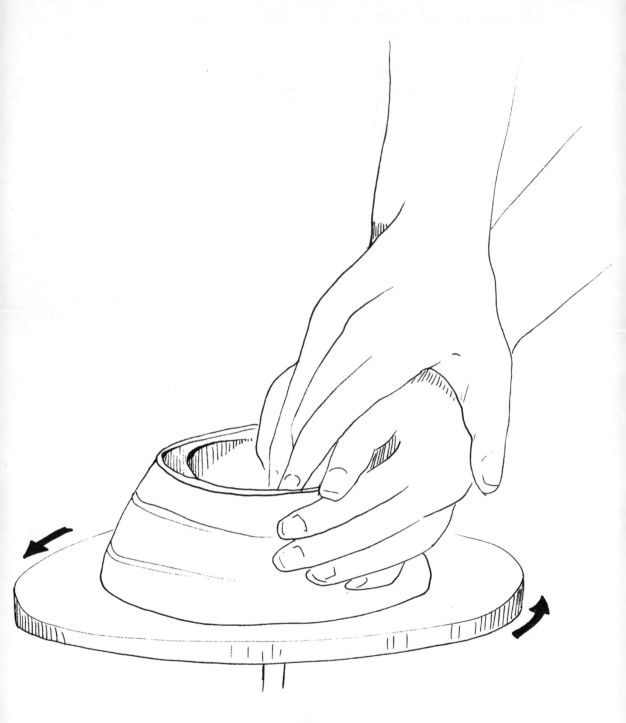

FIG. 43
Opening the clay

FIG. 44
Raising the cylinder

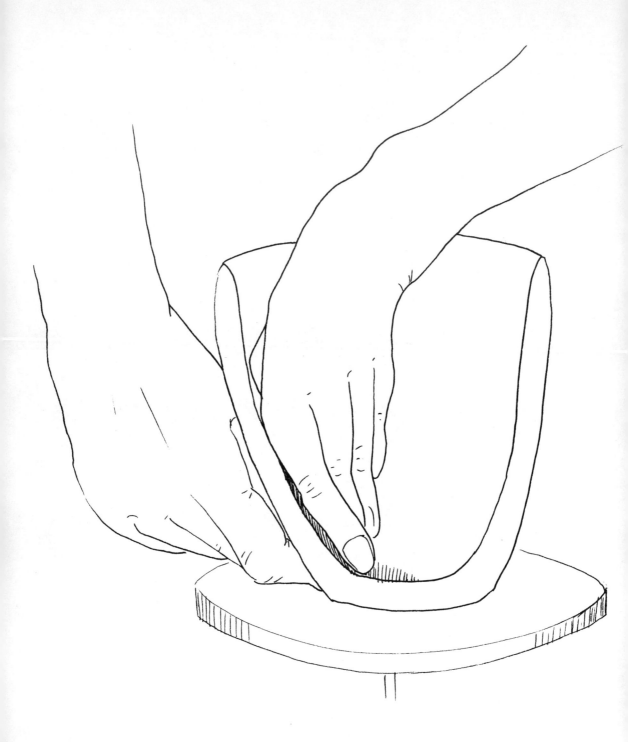

FIG. 45
Cross section of raising a cone

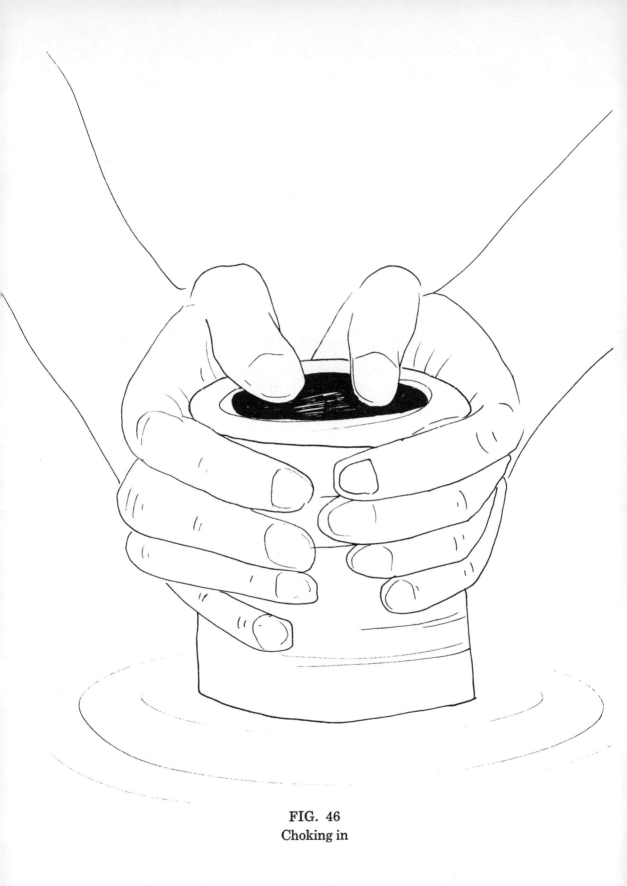

FIG. 46
Choking in

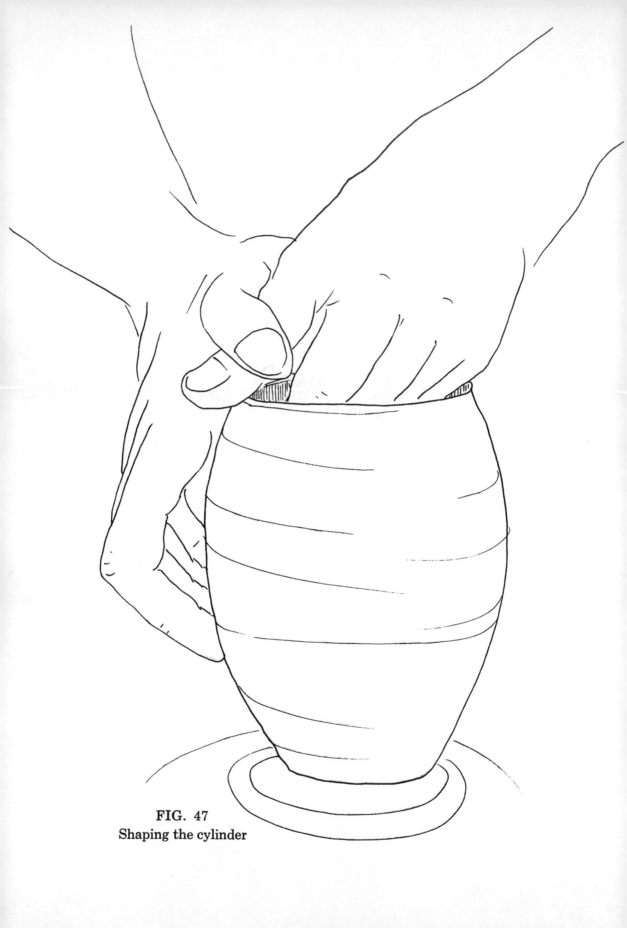

FIG. 47
Shaping the cylinder

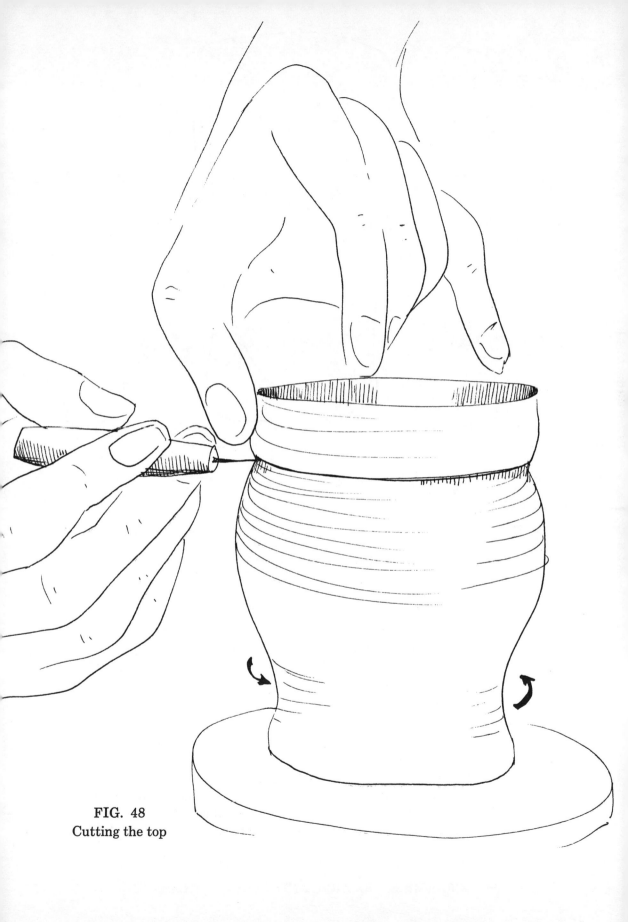

FIG. 48
Cutting the top

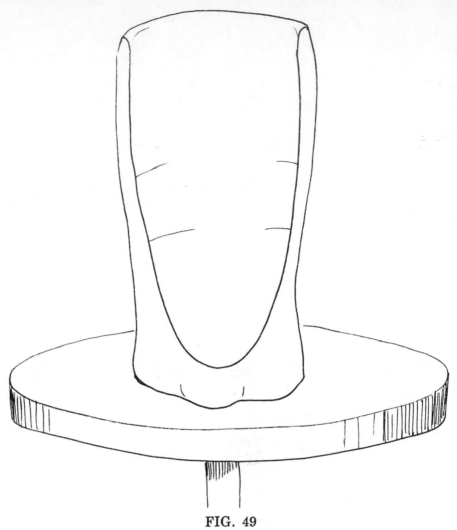

FIG. 49

Cross section showing untrimmed clay at base of piece

(9) Clean the base. After shaping, there is usually excess clay left on the wheel at the base of the piece (Fig. 49). While the wheel is turning, remove this with a wooden modeling tool (Fig. 50). Take care that the tool does not dig into the base of the piece or scratch the bat.

(10) If the piece has been thrown on a plaster bat which will not be needed in the immediate future, remove the bat with the piece on it to the damp box to start the drying process. By the next day the piece will most likely have dried enough to break away from the bat. By that time it will be almost leather hard and can be removed easily by hand. This is the recommended method because it is the safest. However, if the piece must be removed from the bat,

FIG. 50
Trimming base with wooden tool

cut it away with a clay pull (Fig. 51), holding the pull close to the bat and pulling gently but firmly. Obviously, if the pull is not held low enough, the piece will be cut from its base, or the base will be too thin. Remove the piece from the wheel with metal lifters (Fig. 52, Fig. 53) or by hand, using the extra strength of the base for lifting.

(11) Turn the foot. Trim clay from the leather-hard pieces to form a foot. The more carefully done ceramic pieces have a small ridge of clay called a foot. The foot may or may not be a part of the design of the piece (Fig. 54). When the piece has dried to a firm, leather-hard stage, invert it on the wheel head for turning.

With the wheel turning at slow speed and the piece upside down

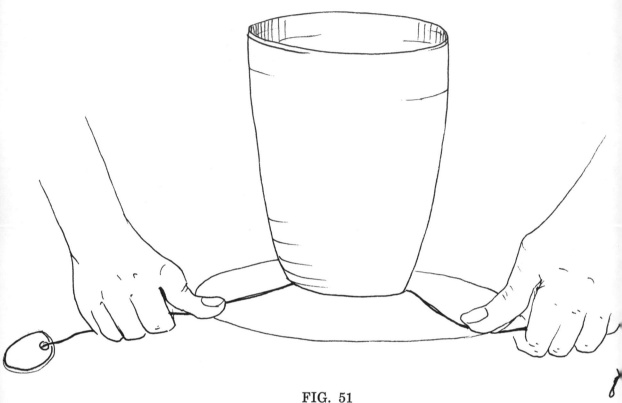

FIG. 51
Cutting the cylinder from the wheel

on the wheel, use a pencil to check for centering. Hold the pencil point close to the piece (Fig. 55). If the pencil bumps at one point, stop the wheel and move the piece away just a little. Continue this checking and moving until the piece is exactly centered on the wheel.

When the piece is exactly centered, secure it to the head or bat with three clay keys placed nearly equidistant around the piece. These keys should be soft enough to hold to the surface of the wheel and form easily around the edge of the piece.

After the piece is centered and secure, turn out a foot for the

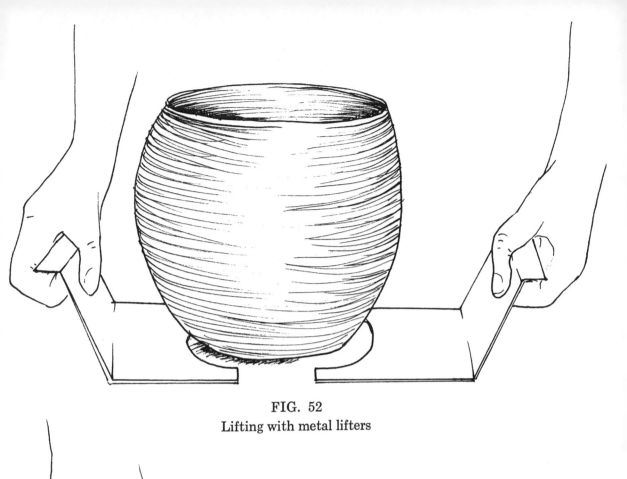

FIG. 52
Lifting with metal lifters

FIG. 53
Lifting by hand

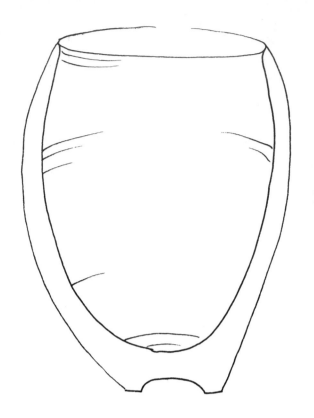

FIG. 54A
Hidden foot rim

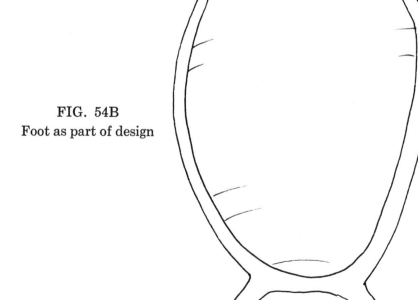

FIG. 54B
Foot as part of design

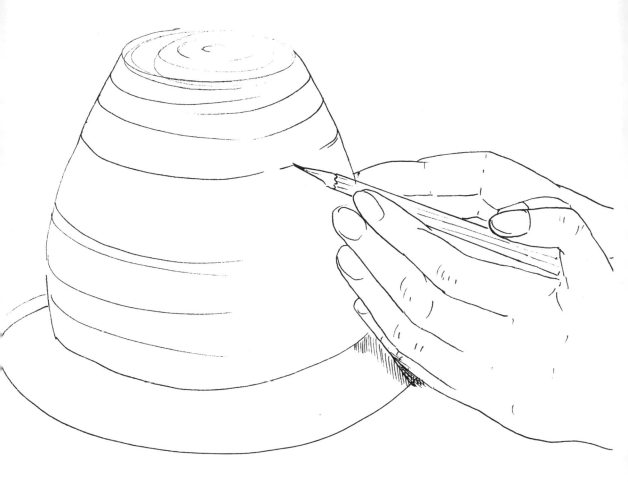

FIG. 55
Testing for centering

piece to rest on. With the hands resting on the edge of the wheel or
on a turning stick, push a loop into the piece very gently to cut
away the excess clay and obtain a foot (Fig. 57A). Cutting several
thin layers rather than one thick one is safest and produces the best
results (Fig. 57B). Care must be taken to keep from cutting
through the base of the piece. Fig. 57C illustrates the completed
piece.

If the piece is completed, set it aside to dry thoroughly. It is
wise to allow it to dry in the inverted position for a while to maintain even moisture content throughout the piece.

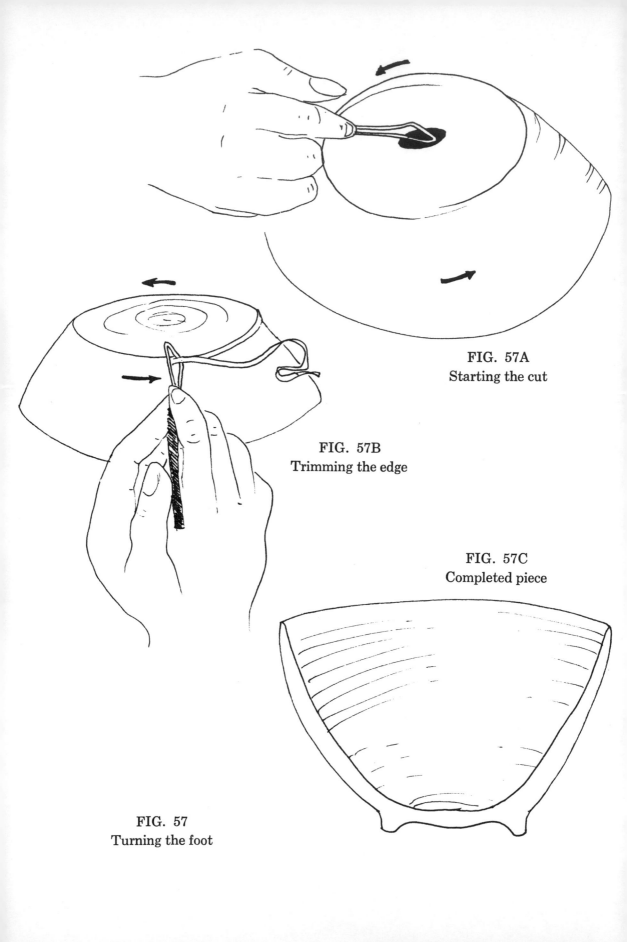

FIG. 57A
Starting the cut

FIG. 57B
Trimming the edge

FIG. 57C
Completed piece

FIG. 57
Turning the foot

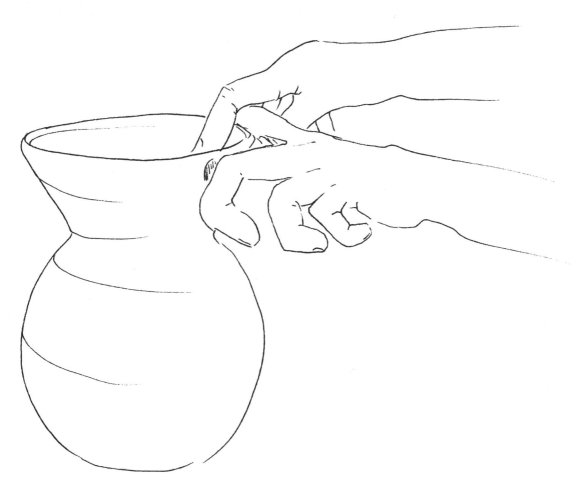

FIG. 58
Forming the spout

(12) Form a spout. The only difference between a shaped cone and a pitcher is a spout and a handle. Both additions are easy to make, and they increase the versatility of the potter's wares. If a spout is to be formed, leave a little extra thickness at the top of the piece. Stop the wheel from turning, but while the piece is still on the wheel and clay is very plastic, form the spout. Wet the hands and press the first two fingers of the left hand against the outside of the piece at the top edge (Fig. 58), and with the index finger of the right hand placed behind these fingers and on the inside of the piece, pull the clay out between the fingers of the left hand. The clay must be pulled and stretched very gently. The marks left by the fingers can be obliterated with a damp sponge.

(13) Make a handle. After the thrown piece has dried for an hour or two, so it will hold its shape a little, apply the handle, which can be either rolled or pulled.

Make a rolled handle from a coil of clay and flatten it. Cut it to the right length, rough up the surfaces of the piece and the handle, and attach it with slip or slurry.

The pulled handle has a better shape, and it usually looks more professional. To make one, grasp a "longish" lump of clay, about the size of an orange, and hold it in the left hand with one end protruding (Fig. 59A). Wet the right hand and gradually pull or "milk" the protruding end into a somewhat flattened piece, tapering down from the size of the lump of clay in the left hand to nearly a point at the end. The clay must be coaxed into the desired shape by squeezing—a pulling motion (Fig. 59A) repeated over the length a dozen or more times. When the clay is thin enough for a handle, it will be very pliable. Turn the clay up, and the clay tail will bend of its own weight into a graceful loop (Fig. 59A). Set it aside to harden for 2 or 3 hours. When the clay is set, trim it (Fig. 59B) and then attach it to the piece (Fig. 59C). Pulling a handle is a skill which must be developed through practice, but the better shape on a nicely thrown piece is well worth the effort.

SCULPTURING

The true test of artistic craftsmanship in clay is ceramic sculpture.

First consider a suitable clay for modeling. The clay must be plastic enough to be worked with ease, yet firm enough to hold up under its own weight. Most modeling clays are firm enough for small pieces (6″ or so), but for very large pieces, an armature must be used. For good modeling or sculpturing, the clay must be of the right consistency. One test is to press the thumb into the wedged clay. If the clay is sticky, it is too moist and should be rewedged on the plaster side of the wedging board. If cracks appear in the depression of the clay ball, add a little water to moisten the clay, then rewedge it thoroughly.

In constructing a piece of sculpture, be concerned first with only general shaping: Establish the broad masses and values first, and detail can follow. The general shape should be slightly larger than the desired finished size to allow for size lost in shrinkage and in carving clay off to form the piece. Rotate the piece and view it from various angles as work progresses, for sculpturing embodies

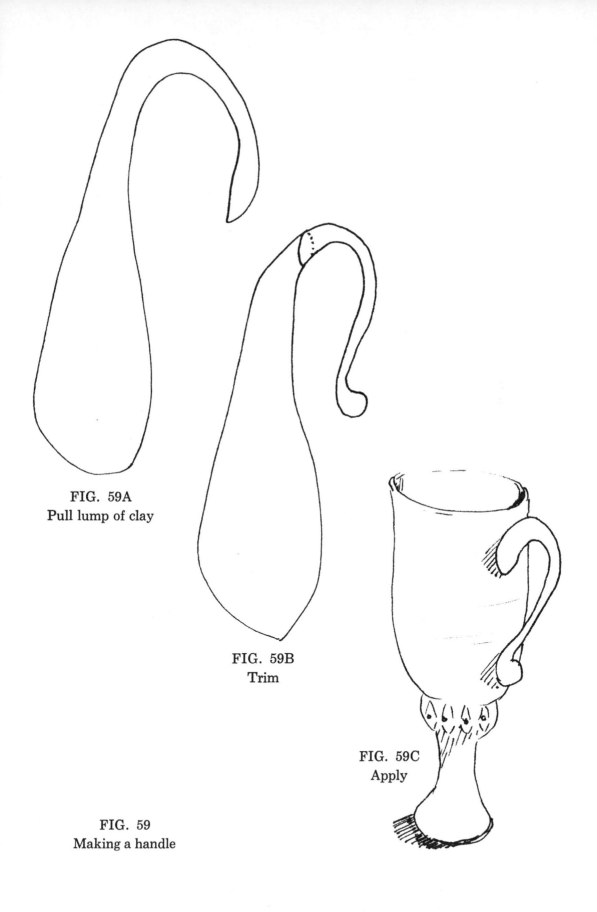

FIG. 59A
Pull lump of clay

FIG. 59B
Trim

FIG. 59C
Apply

FIG. 59
Making a handle

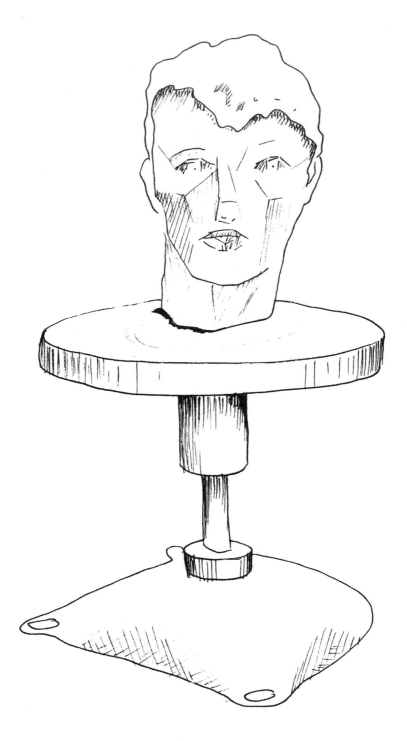

FIG. 60
Sculpture without armature

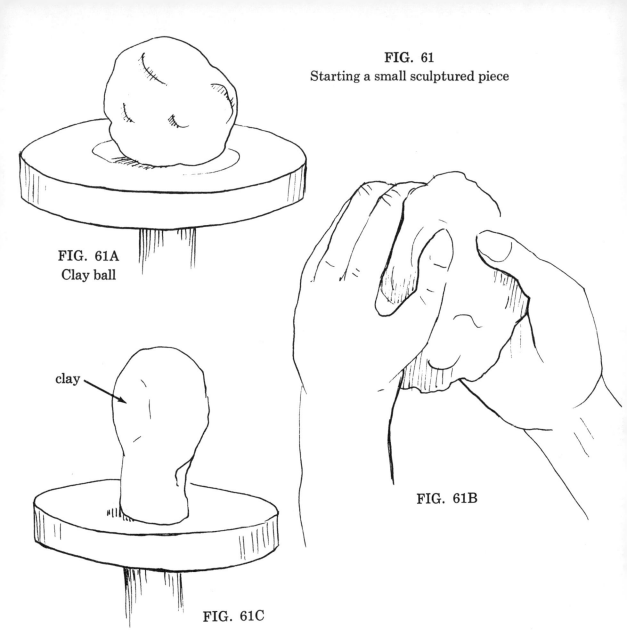

FIG. 61
Starting a small sculptured piece

FIG. 61A
Clay ball

clay

FIG. 61B

FIG. 61C

three dimensions. It is frequently helpful to work on a decorating wheel, which provides for easy turning of the piece.

Small bulky sculptured pieces to approximately 6″ tall are usually sturdy enough to support their own weight and do not need an armature for added support (Fig. 60).

To make a small basic piece that will not require an armature, shape well-wedged clay into a ball approximately the size of an orange (Fig. 61A). Then squeeze and press it with both hands and slowly form it into a simple rhythmic shape (Fig. 61B). From this point, the figure or shape of the piece is left to the imagination and dexterity of the sculptor, who is free to model the clay

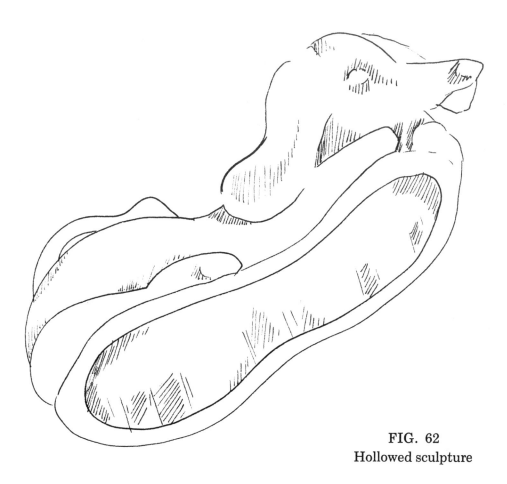

FIG. 62
Hollowed sculpture

into anything he desires, such as an animal, bust, bowl, or abstract figure. Sculpturing is done mainly with the hands, aided by a few modeling tools. The piece must be hollowed out (Fig. 62) to have a wall ¼″ to ½″ thick, to speed drying and to keep it from exploding during the firing process.

Pieces requiring armatures are generally busts or action poses of figures. In some shapes, the clay cannot support its own weight. For example, if you want to make a slender figure with the arms reaching outward, the body and arms will have to be supported during the modeling, or the clay will collapse. For this type of sculpturing, use an armature of pipe and wire (Fig. 63A). The armature might also be a simple upright piece of wood (Fig. 63B) or a plastic bag filled with sand and then tied (Fig. 63C); the sand is removed upon completion of the project by opening the bag and draining the sand, then removing the plastic bag.

FIG. 63
Types of armatures

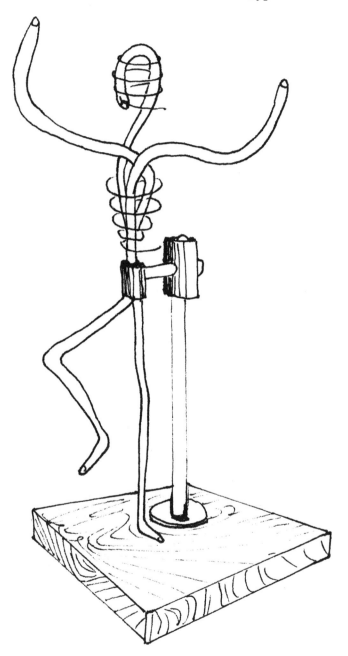

FIG. 63A
Pipe and wire

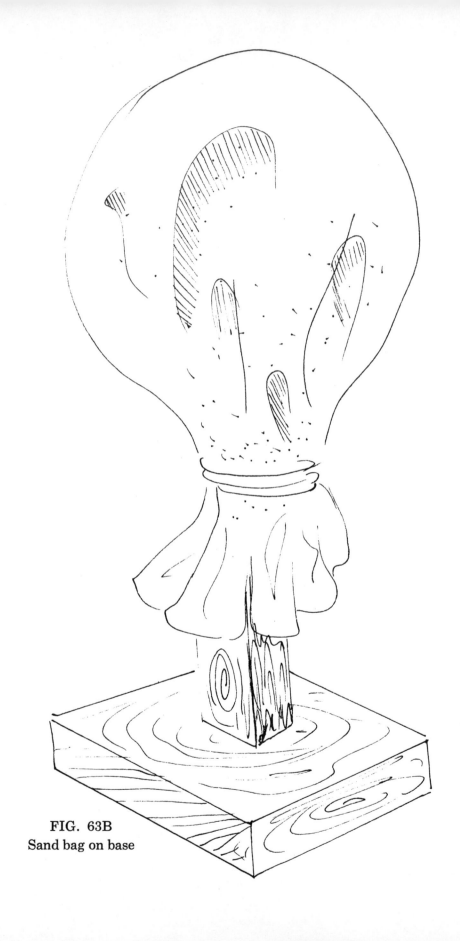

FIG. 63B
Sand bag on base

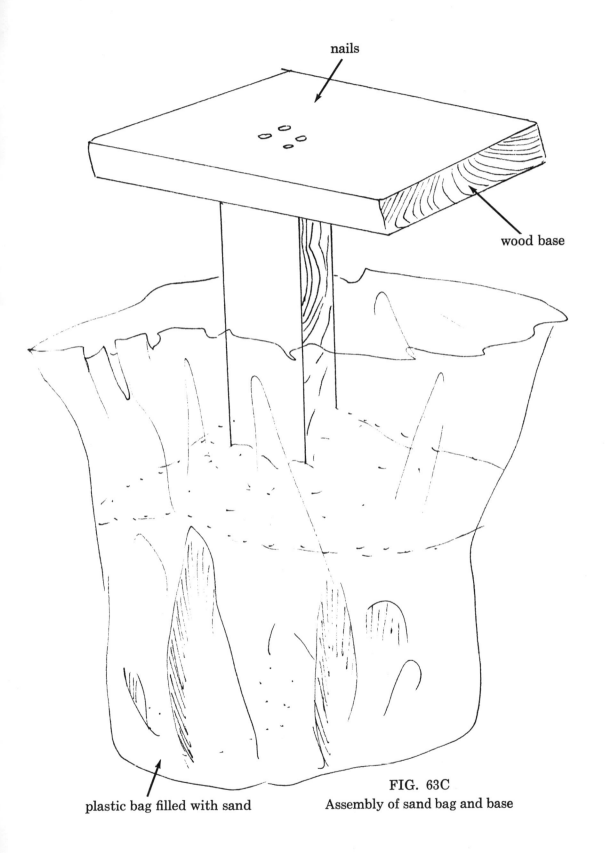

nails

wood base

plastic bag filled with sand

FIG. 63C
Assembly of sand bag and base

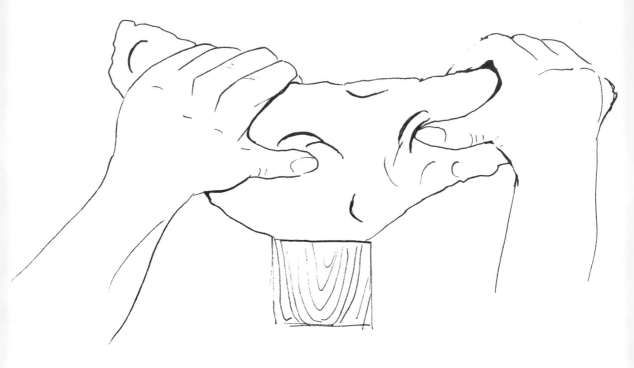

FIG. 64
Rough shaping of clay

For the sake of simplicity, doing a bust over a sandbag armature
will be considered. In this project, most techniques are used:
the use of the armature; hand forming; shaping with wooden
blocks, mallets, and modeling tools. The first step in modeling a
bust is to form an appropriate amount of wedged clay around the
upright piece of wood containing the sandbag on the armature.
Then, with hands opposing one another, press the clay into roughly
the desired shape. After rough shaping with the hands, use wooden
blocks or a mallet for pushing or pounding the clay into shape
(Fig. 65). When the roughing cut has been completed and the large
masses are shaped, more modeling detail begins. This work is done
with the fingers, mainly the thumb. If the thumb becomes weary,

FIG. 65
Rough shaping with block of wood

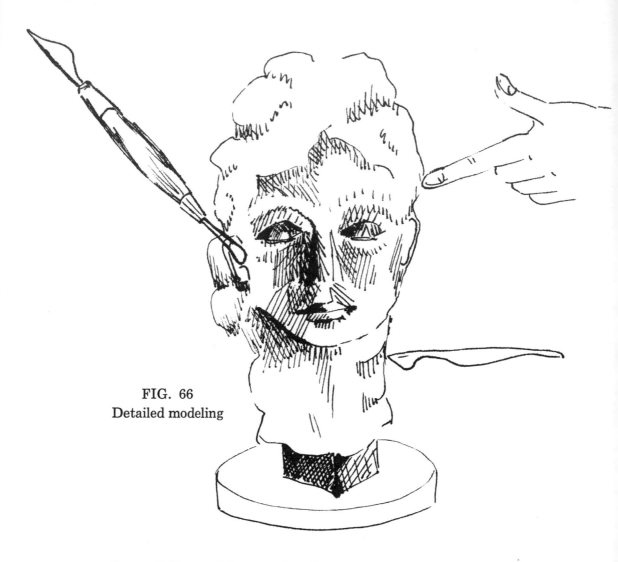

FIG. 66
Detailed modeling

the modeling tool is a good replacement (Fig. 66). This modeling
tool, with its broad, slightly curved surface, is useful for pressing
on additional lumps of clay to build up the form. The next step is
the final detail and finishing of surfaces, and wire loop tools in
various shapes are useful for removing excess clay—for example,
around the eyes and the nose (Fig. 66). This sculpturing and
shading may take days or even weeks to complete. When the clay
is not being worked on, it must be kept moist with wet towels and
plastic. Upon completion, smooth the surface with a damp sponge
and set the piece aside to dry slowly and evenly to leather hard.
Then remove the armature by untying the string or binding holding the sand and removing the wooden post and plastic bag. Let
the piece dry thoroughly and evenly until it is bone dry and
ready to fire.

MOLD MAKING AND SLIP-CASTING

Mold making and slip-casting are discussed together because in practice they are inseparable. The molds into which clay slip is poured are made of plaster of paris. Utmost care must be taken in making molds in order to have good results in the process of slip-casting.

MOLD MAKING

Depending upon the shape of the piece being reproduced, molds may be simple one-piece devices, or they may be very complex with many pieces fitting together. The beginner should attempt to reproduce a simple shape, one that requires no more than a two-piece mold. A shape with undercuts requires a mold which separates laterally. It can be reproduced in a two-piece mold if the bottom is flat, rather than footed. A shape to be reproduced may be made from plaster, modeled from oil-base clay, or taken from a ready-made piece. Because of the shrinkage of clay a mold will produce a duplicate a little smaller than the original. The following steps are used in making a two-piece mold:

(1) Cut a template to fit the profile of the piece exactly. To do this, draw center lines on opposite sides of the model, dividing it exactly in half. This can be done with a T-square (Fig. 67). The template must fit this marked line. The template may be cut from heavy cardboard, which is then coated with three coats of shellac and sized with soap.

(2) Lay the template on soft clay; then put the model in place so that it is embedded exactly to the center line. Fill any space between the template and the model with clay to secure a perfect fit (Fig. 68).

(3) Out of clay, make a plug to fit ½" beyond the top rim of the mold. Pouring will be easier if the plug is a little larger at the top, as the slip must be poured in and drained out of the opening left by the plug.

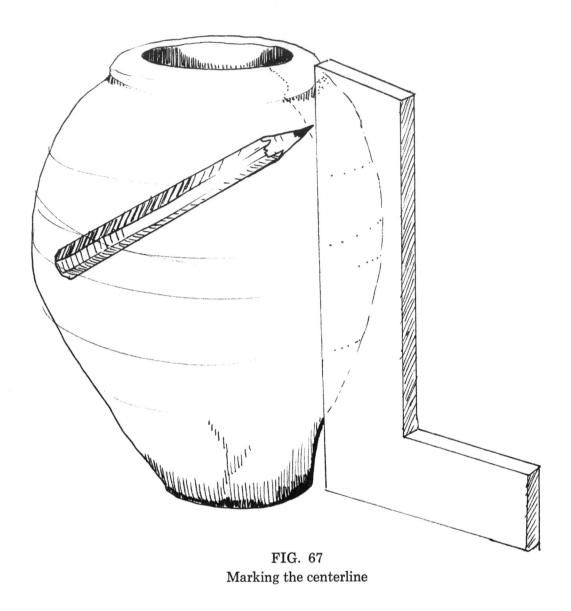

FIG. 67
Marking the centerline

(4) After the plug is in place, size the model, set the casting box around the clay, and size the box (see page 35).

(5) Make a casting box. A simple, adjustable frame for casting rectangular shapes is made from four pieces of ¾″ lumber about 6″ wide and 15″ long. Each piece of lumber has a piece of strap iron screwed to one end (Fig. 69). There, the four pieces of wood fit together to make a box of any size up to 15″ square. Four wedges are used to hold them tightly while the plaster is poured.

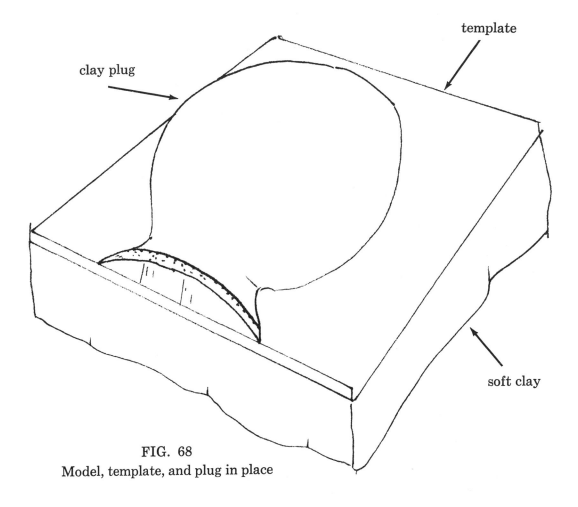

clay plug

template

soft clay

FIG. 68
Model, template, and plug in place

(6) Mix enough plaster to nearly fill the remaining space in the casting box, and pour the plaster into the box (see page 32).

(7) When the plaster has set, turn the box over and remove the clay backing and the template, but keep the model in the mold.

(8) Put another plug of clay at the top of the model; cut notches in the first half of the mold (two on one side and one on the other side); size the mold, the model, and the casting box; then pour the second half of the mold.

(9) After the plaster sets, remove the box and plug and gently separate the two halves of the mold. The mold is completed (Fig. 70) and can be used when it is thoroughly dry.

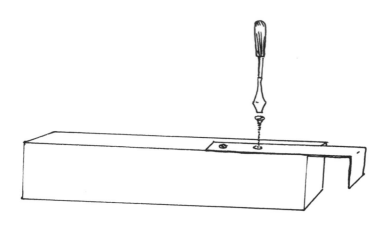

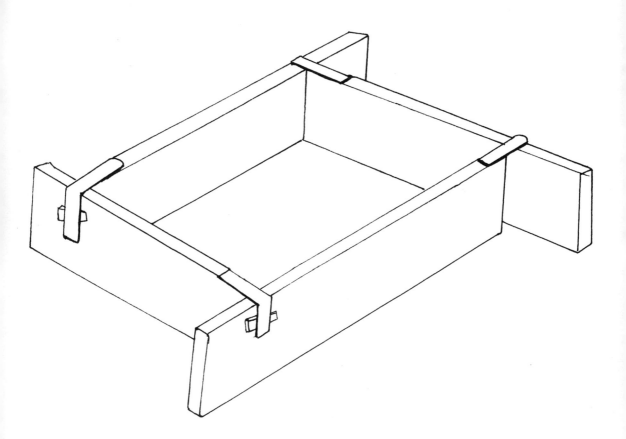

FIG. 69
Assembly of casting box (not wedges)

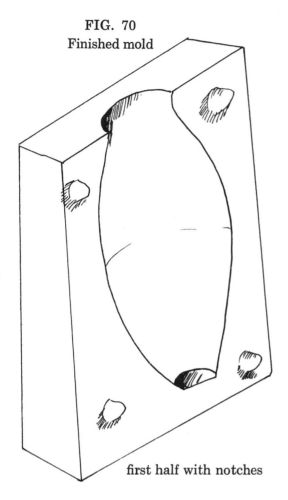

FIG. 70
Finished mold

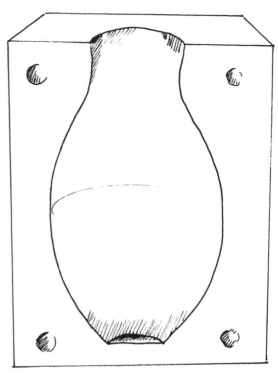

second half with indentations

first half with notches

Molds require care because plaster is not a sturdy material and any scratch or nick in the plaster will be reproduced in the casting. If molds are dried thoroughly after each use, they work more satisfactorily because the absorption of water is more rapid.

After the molds are used, clean them. It is easier, and best for the mold, to clean the clay off before it hardens. The clay can be taken off the outside of the mold with a fettling knife, but care must be taken not to scratch the mold. A damp sponge or kidney-shaped rubber is an excellent tool to use for cleaning a mold, as neither will scratch the surface.

Wipe the working surface with a damp (not wet) sponge. If this does not remove all of the clay, rub gently with an old nylon stocking.

Dry the mold as rapidly as possible so that it will be ready to use again. It will dry more rapidly if it is left unassembled. It must not be heated over 120° F., as plaster does not stand up at higher temperatures.

When the parts of the mold are completely dry, assemble them, using rubber bands to hold them together, and store the mold where it will not get bumped. *Note:* Molds do wear out after repeated use, but good care is very important in prolonging their usefulness.

SLIP-CASTING

The fundamental principles which make this process possible are interesting. Plaster is porous, and it absorbs water quite rapidly. As the water from the slip is absorbed, the clay suspended in the water is deposited on the surface of the plaster. When this deposit of clay is sufficiently thick, the remaining slip is poured from the center of the mold so that no more deposit is made. Absorption and evaporation serve to remove the water from the deposit until the volume of the deposit lessens and it becomes smaller in size and pulls away from the plaster. The following steps are used in slip-casting:

(1) When the mold is thoroughly dry, it is ready for slip-casting. A mold can be held together in one of several ways; perhaps the most satisfactory is with rubber bands made by cutting slices of an inner tube to a width of ¾" or 1".

(2) Make the prepared slip ready for use by mixing it well and straining it so there will be no lumps. Put the slip in a container which will hold enough to fill the mold.

(3) Pour a steady stream of slip into the center of the mold until it is level with the top. Tap the mold a little with the hand so that any air bubbles will rise to the top.

(4) As water is absorbed by the plaster, the level of the slip in the mold will go down, so add more slip to keep the mold full to the top of the waste rim.

(5) The longer the slip stays in the mold, the thicker the sides of the piece being molded will be. It is not possible to guess ac-

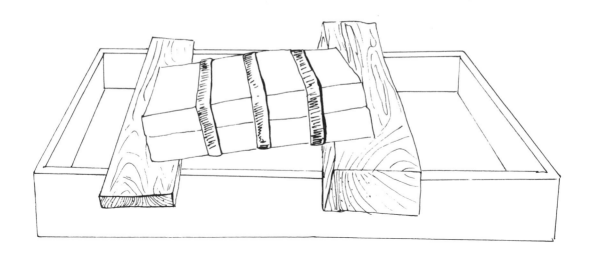

FIG. 71
Draining a mold

curately how long the slip should remain in the mold, because the consistency of the slip, the dryness of the mold, and the humidity in the air all have a bearing on the rate at which water is absorbed by plaster. To determine the thickness of the deposit, cut into the deposit on the waste rim which was formed on the mold by the plug of clay. Continue checking in a different spot each time until the deposit of clay is of the desired thickness.

(6) The liquid slip must then be poured from the center of the mold. To do this, take the mold in both hands and, while holding it over a bowl or pitcher, rotate the mold with a slow, steady motion until it is nearly upside down. Hold it for a few minutes (do *not* shake it) until most of the slip has run out; then rest the mold on two sticks of different height, which are placed over a container (Fig. 71). Tip the mold during the final draining to prevent drops of slip from forming on the bottom of the mold. If a mug with a handle is being drained, it is often advisable to let it drain with the handle at the bottom so that the drained slip will fill up the indentations otherwise formed where the handle meets the mold.

(7) When the shine disappears from its surface, the slip is starting to dry and the mold may be turned up. Clean the slip from the edges of the mold at this time.

(8) As the casting dries, it will begin to pull away from the mold. It is good to loosen carefully any part which sticks, so the drying will be even. Allow the piece to dry until it is largely pulled away from the mold. This may take an hour or two. Cut the waste rim off the piece and put it with the scrap slip to be reclaimed.

(9) The best time to remove the piece from the mold is determined mainly from experience. It must be sufficiently dry to maintain its shape out of the mold. Remove one half of the mold first and let the piece dry in the other half a little longer before removing it.

(10) While the casting is leather hard, scrape off the seam marks with a fettling knife and smooth them with a damp elephant-ear sponge. Smooth the top rim also by rubbing it over a piece of sandpaper or glass which is on the flat tabletop. Smooth the edge with an elephant-ear sponge, and set the piece aside to dry.

STORAGE AND DRYING OF CLAY
AND PROJECTS

For clay to stay plastic and workable, it must be kept moist. Unshaped clay is stored in a rustproof container with a tight-fitting cover. A large crock with a lid is excellent. For temporary storage, clay can be wrapped in wet cloth and kept in a plastic bag.

Projects which have been started and are to be worked on again can be carefully wrapped in wet cloths, slipped into a plastic bag, and stored in the damp box. If they are not worked on for several days, the cloths may have to be dampened again. Work stored in the damp box must be kept covered with a wet cloth if it is to remain plastic. Uncovered, pieces will gradually dry to leather hard. In this state, the clay is too dry to be plastic but can be carved without chipping.

When work on a project is complete, it must be dried slowly, evenly, and thoroughly. Drying should be started in the damp box. Leave the piece uncovered in the box until it is leather hard. Open shelves in a comfortably warm room, out of the sunlight and away from drafts, is the next step. Put the project on them to finish drying.

Drying must take place evenly throughout the project or the difference in volume of the clay, caused by greater loss of moisture in one area, will make cracks appear. Since the base of a piece on a solid shelf will dry more slowly than the top, turn the piece over as often as necessary to keep the drying even. This is particularly important when making tiles. They must be turned every few hours to prevent warping. Use special care with such projects as sculptured pieces, pitchers, and cups which have slender protuberances that dry more rapidly than the rest of the piece. To keep the drying even, hang small wet cloths over the areas which might dry too rapidly. These bits of cloth must be redampened as they dry.

SURFACE COLORING AND FINISHING

TYPES

Underglaze is a mixture of ceramic materials compounded for use on green or bisque ware. Although pieces decorated with underglaze may be fired and left as bisque, a transparent glaze usually is applied over the entire surface to enhance the appearance, strengthen the piece, and waterproof it. The popularity of underglaze decoration stems from the fact that it makes almost any type of design possible—from the most delicate brush stroke to a solid background of color. Underglazes can be painted, sprayed, sponged, or spattered, with endless variations and combinations possible in each technique. Before the underglaze is applied, it must be stirred thoroughly. It must also be stirred at frequent intervals during use in order to maintain maximum color strength, or the pigments will settle to the bottom of the container. Only by trial and error can one determine the exact amount of underglaze to be applied. Underglaze has a water base and will dry when exposed to air, so it should be stored in an airtight jar. If glaze becomes too thick, the consistency can be restored by adding a little water. Underglazes may be purchased in prepared liquid form, which is ready to use, or in powdered form, to which water is added. If underglazes are to be used in quantity, they are less expensive to purchase in powder form.

Glaze is a thin coating of glass which fuses to the surface of a clay body during firing. It provides strength and beauty and is impervious to moisture and dirt. Glaze comes in decorative textures and permanent colors, and it provides a cover for underglaze decoration. Different glazes are made to fire at different temperatures; each is indicated on the container.

Majolica glazes are brilliant, opaque, transparent colors which may be applied to green or bisque ware. They are available in liquid or powder form. These glazes will produce a rich, shiny surface which flows slightly and thereby corrects irregularities of the brush application. Crawling, running, and separating of colors are common difficulties with Majolica glaze, but these problems can be overcome by proper application of the glaze, correct handling of the ware, and controlled firing. Each make of glaze may have a different firing temperature. The recommended cone firing for each glaze is found on the container or provided by the distributor.

Mat glaze fires with a soft, dull finish. It is particularly effective on contemporary or traditional shapes with simple lines. Mat glaze flows enough to cover most application defects, but not as much as Majolica glaze. Because of this nonflowing quality, mat glazes are adaptable for some unique types of decorations, both alone and in combination with other glazes. They may be applied by spray, brush, or dipping, as with other glazes. Mat glaze may be purchased in ready-to-use liquid form or in dry powder to which water is added.

Crackle glaze is made to craze as it cools. Decorative effects may be obtained from the patterns of the fine lines which develop in the glaze. The crackle is most prominent in the light, transparent glaze colors, but less apparent in the opaque. Rubbing light- or dark-colored inks into the fine lines accentuates the crackle. This is done after the piece has been removed from the kiln and while it is still warm. Brushing, dipping, and spraying are suitable methods for applying crackle glaze to green or bisque ware. The glaze may be purchased in liquid form in various colors.

Opalescent glazes are so named because, in addition to the gloss, they have an opal or mother-of-pearl quality, rather than the plain color of some other glazes. Opalescent glaze may be used on any fine art clay, but it develops its greatest opalescence and most interesting texture when used over red clays. It is applied to bisque or green ware by brush or by dipping, pouring, or spraying. On red bisque, these glazes should be applied rather heavily. A slow, rather than fast, firing is best.

No two pieces glazed with alligator glaze are ever alike, because of the many variations in texture that occur in firing. Varied mat textures are predominant at low-firing temperatures, gloss textures at higher temperatures, and a mingling of mat and gloss between extremes. A crepelike texture is characteristic, and the entire piece is enriched with warm undertones. It is applied as other glazes and purchased in liquid ready-to-use or dry powder form.

Speckle glaze has a multicolor speckled finish. Because of the presence of the specks, it is *not* suitable for spraying. Approximately three heavy coats are recommended for application. Speckled glazes are purchased in a variety of colors in liquid form only.

Wood glaze is a realistic-looking "wood finish" glaze applied rather heavily by a brush in long strokes or with a cloth to green ware or bisque to grain the surface being glazed. Wood glazes are available in liquid form only, in seven different types: hickory, walnut, mahogany, redwood, fruitwood, driftwood, and birch.

Overglaze decorations are painted on ceramic pieces which have been glazed and fired. After the overglaze is applied, the piece is allowed to dry. Then it is put in the kiln and fired just high enough to allow the glaze to soften slightly so that the colors become locked in the glaze. The correct firing temperature is indicated on the container. During firing, the glaze does not run, so one color may be brushed on top of another and the colors may be blended to get intermediary tones. Overglaze comes in liquid form only in a variety of colors.

Salt glazing is an interesting type of decoration which is accomplished entirely in the ring process. This method of glazing was discovered by German potters in the 15th century, and it is still done there. It was used in America in the 19th century to produce utilitarian pieces such as crocks, churns, and jugs. Salt-glazed pieces are often decorated with a blue engobe. Green ware is placed in the kiln and fired to the maturing temperature of the clay. At that temperature, salt is thrown into the fire box of the kiln. The salt vaporizes in the heat of the kiln and combines with the silica of the clay to form a thin, mat glaze over the pieces in the kiln. A downdraft kiln, open fired, is preferable for salt glazing, but it must be vented into a chimney to prevent the fumes (chlorine gas) from escaping inside the building. This type of glazing is *not* done in an electric kiln. After repeated firings, the entire inside of the firing chamber becomes coated with glaze. Most ordinary clays will salt-glaze successfully.

Bisque stains are applied to bisque ware that has been fired no higher than cone 06 (a higher temperature will mature the clay so that it will not absorb the stain). The piece is not refired after the stain is applied. Bisque stain is used to decorate items such as figurines, boxes, and wall plaques. It should not be used for items such as cups, bowls, and dishes, as bisque absorbs liquids and the stain is water soluble. Stains of different colors can be mixed like paint; for example, blue and yellow can be mixed to make green. Colors of stain are true as they come from the jar, and they do not change as fired glazes do. When dry, the stain is bright and lusterless. To get a shiny finish, a spray-fix mat or clear lacquer is applied. Some possibilities of decorating with stain are antiquing and woodgraining.

pour to here

FIG. 72A
Glazing inside of piece

GLAZING METHODS

Pouring is perhaps the most satisfactory method of glazing the inside of hollow pieces such as vases and pitchers. The consistency of the glaze must be controlled in order to have the correct thickness deposited on the piece. Dense bodies absorb little or no water; therefore, the glaze used on more matured clay must be thicker than that used on porous, less matured pieces.

To glaze the inside, pour *more* than enough glaze to cover the area (Fig. 72A); then slowly rotate the piece to deposit the glaze evenly, pouring the excess glaze out and back into the glaze container (Fig. 72B). Outside surfaces can be glazed by pouring the glaze over them (Fig. 73).

The spraying method is good for glazing large pieces. Spraying tends to deposit a more even coating of glaze, it is faster, and only enough glaze to cover the piece is required. An air compressor, a paint sprayer, a ventilated spray booth, and a revolving table are equipment necessary for spray glazing. The glaze is sprayed by air pressure in a regular paint sprayer at high velocity onto the surface of the bisque ware. Spray-gun nozzles differ, so the exact distance cannot be predetermined. If the gun is held too far away, the glaze will dry before it hits the piece, and loose, fluffy glaze will be deposited. If the sprayer is held too close or held too long in one place, the glaze deposit becomes too wet, and it will run (Fig. 74). The person using the sprayer must wear a protective mask to prevent inhalation of glaze, which can be harmful after a period of time.

Dipping is used for production work because it is possible to obtain an even coating of glaze quickly. For the studio potter, however, it is usually impractical because of the large amount of glaze required. To prevent too heavy a coating, the piece must be wiped with a damp sponge, then quickly immersed in a container of glaze large and deep enough to cover the entire piece. To avoid surface air bubbles, slowly dip the piece in and out of the glaze. After the piece is dipped it should be placed on a screen to drain and dry.

In the brushing method, the glaze is applied with a flat 1" glaze brush. The creamy glaze should be flowed on, rather than brushed. Three layers are usually recommended. The strokes of the second coat are made perpendicular to those of the first and third. More care must be taken to ensure an even application if nonflowing glaze is used. Brushing has the advantage of requiring only a small amount of glaze.

DEFECTS IN GLAZES. There is always an element of uncertainty when firing glazes. Many things can go wrong, and the source of trouble is sometimes hard to trace. It may lie in the glaze or in the way the ingredients were weighed. There may be faults in applying or in firing. About 90 percent of the defects are due to mechanical error, and 10 percent to chemical error. A few of the most common glaze defects and some of the things which cause them are discussed below.

Crazing is one of the most common defects. When a glaze crazes, it develops tiny cracks over the surface. Sometimes these show

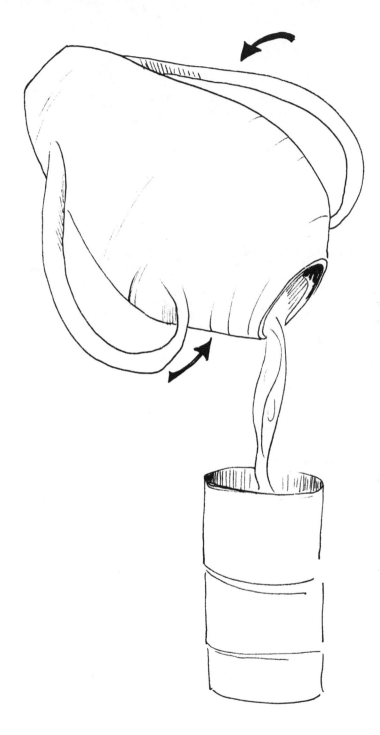

FIG. 72B
Rotate

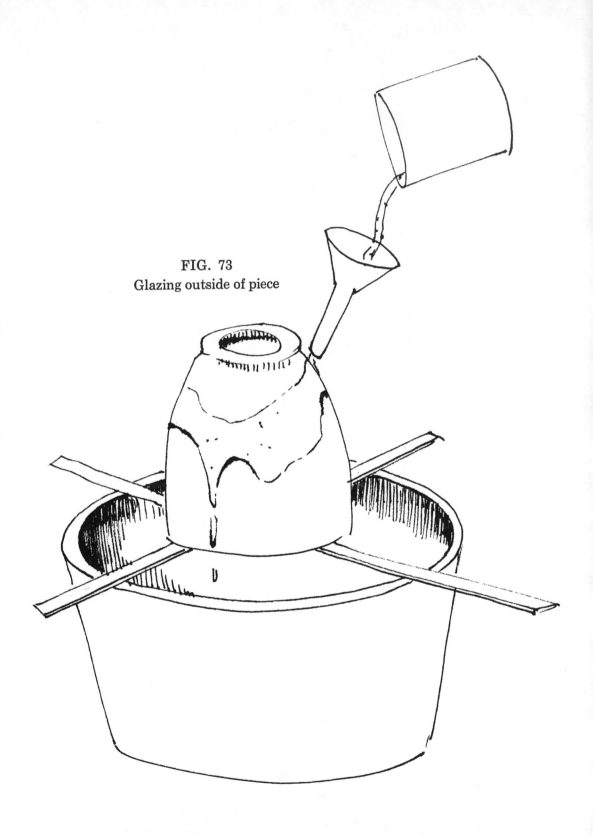

FIG. 73
Glazing outside of piece

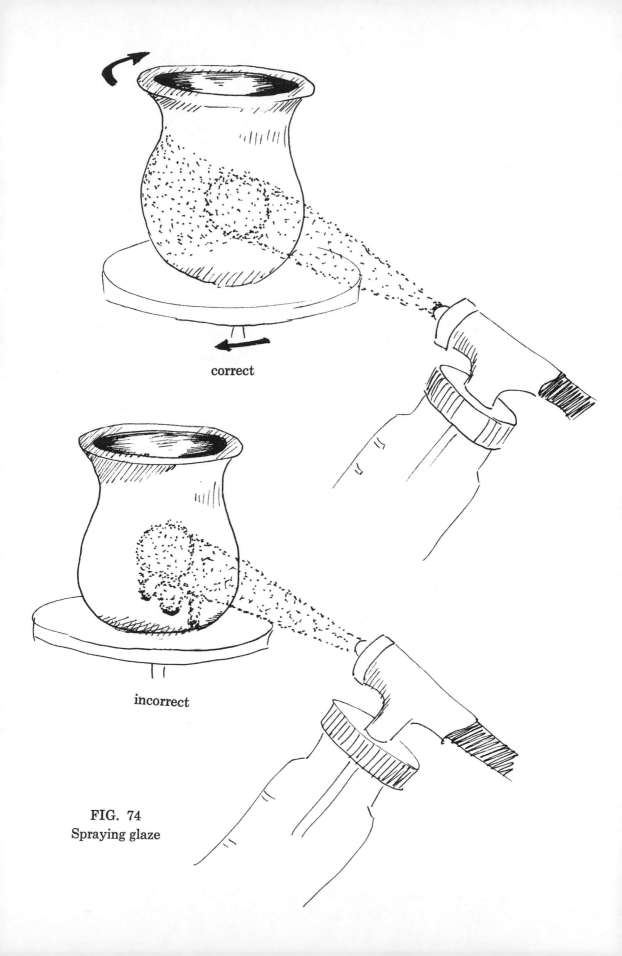

correct

incorrect

FIG. 74
Spraying glaze

immediately after the piece comes out of the kiln, but often they do not appear until several months later. Crazing indicates that the glaze and the body have a different coefficient of expansion. If the ware is fired again at a higher temperature, the crazing will often be corrected.

Crawling occurs when a piece comes out of the kiln with bare spots where the glaze has moved away, exposing the body underneath. Some of the causes of crawling are dust or oil from the fingers on the ware before it was glazed, too heavy an application of glaze, underfiring, firing before the glaze was completely dry, or the use of too porous a clay body for the type of glaze used.

Blisters or craters are formed on the surface of the glaze from too heavy an application of glaze, firing damp glaze, too low firing, or too fast firing.

Tiny holes or pits in the glaze are referred to as pinholes. They are often caused by air holes in the clay, especially in cast pieces. Other causes are too rapid firing or too rapid cooling. Painting over a glaze after it has dried may also cause this trouble.

Too much flux in the glaze will cause the colors to run. Some underglazes add an extra amount of flux to a glaze, causing certain colors to run more than others. If a clear glaze which has not had all of the impurities removed (is not fritted) is applied over underglaze, it will run.

Dryness in a glaze means a rough surface, rather than a smooth, glossy one. Underfiring, not enough flux, or not enough glaze put on the piece will cause dryness.

Shivering refers to sections of glaze lifting off the piece. It is usually caused by an incompatibility between the clay and the glaze. Purchasing the glaze and clay from the same source should eliminate the problem. Another cause of shivering may be too rapid firing or too rapid cooling.

Occasionally the glaze does not produce the color that it should. This may be due to the presence of chromium in the kiln, such as in a chromium green underglaze. Odd bits of stray colors are due to careless handling and are called "tramp color."

CERAMIC DESIGN

The interrelationship of form, texture, and decoration should be considered in ceramic design. In this medium, more than in any other, the sense of touch is included with the eyes and the imagination in the enjoyment of a piece. For instance, a drinking mug should be well balanced, comfortable to hold, and easy to drink from. This quality in ceramics is as important as, and it is dependent upon, the shape, color, and texture of the piece.

The four basic forms (cone, sphere, cube, cylinder) are seen repeatedly, but with myriads of variations and combinations. Because of the nature of the material, ceramic pieces are not slender and willowy, but tend to be more rounded and bulky. One sculptor of note tried to design his pieces so that if they were rolled, no part would break off. This need for more compact roundness does not preclude graceful, clean lines, however.

Texturing of ceramics may be obtained by putting grog in the clay; by using different glazes; by rolling the clay on textured material such as burlap; or by marking the surface with a comb, fork, screen edge, ridged paddle, bisque, stamps, etc. The texturing should be appropriate to the shape and to the intended use of the piece. Deep, narrow grooves in the clay provide interesting texture that is appropriate to a flower pot, for instance, but not to a dinner plate.

Decoration can be put on the clay with underglazing, slip-painting, coils, slip-trailing, running glaze, and wax resist or by scratching the clay. The decoration should relate to the shape and function of the piece. The Egyptians did this well by planning the decorating to accent the shape of the clay. Small motifs were used at the base and the neck of urns; and larger, more important figures were put along the widest area. Decoration can accent an area or perhaps break up a plain area; it can be symbolic, pretty, humorous, or abstract; or it can carry a message.

DECORATING

There are many ways of decorating ceramic pieces in all three forms—green ware, bisque, or glazed. When a piece of clay has not been fired, it is said to be green ware. Green ware is very fragile and will turn into slip if it contacts water. The firing transforms the green ware into what is known as bisque (or biscuit) ware. Bisque is sufficiently hard and durable to require no processing, but it is rough, dull, and porous. Glazing puts a glasslike coating on the piece, making it smooth, nonporous, and waterproof.

DECORATION ON GREEN WARE

The design can be carved directly into the leather-hard clay as in wood carving. A knife such as a fettling knife is used.

Liquid rubber (rubber latex) can be used in place of wax as a resist material. One of the advantages of rubber is that, unlike wax, no bisque firing is required to burn the rubber out. The liquid rubber is removed by prying up its edge with a sharp tool and peeling it off. This means that the piece can be glazed and fired in a single operation. If the rubber latex becomes a little thick for the brush work, it can be thinned with diluted ammonia. Ammonia is also used to clean the brush immediately after use.

Slip is usually applied as a form of decoration in one of the following manners.

Painting: Colored slip (engobe) is applied to leather-hard clay with a brush.

Slip-trailing: Thick slip is applied to leather-hard clay with a tracing tube or cake decorator. This leaves the design in a ridge of clay, either to match the body or to contrast with it.

Sgraffito: A thin coat of slip of a contrasting color is applied over the surface of the leather-hard piece. After it dries, a design is scratched through the colored slip to expose the base color beneath.

Mishima: Leather-hard green ware is incised with a design, and then a slip of a contrasting color is painted over the incising. After the top layer dries, it is scraped off, leaving the contrasting slip in the design.

Airbrush: Slip decoration is applied by use of stencils and a spray gun. The same effect can be obtained by spattering colored slip on the piece instead of spraying it.

Sponge: Instead of a brush being used to put designs on either green or bisque ware, applying the color with a sponge provides a nice change. A sponge is dipped into slip and dabbed on the piece; interesting color combinations as well as textures can be obtained this way.

Stencils: The desired pattern is cut out of paper; then color is dabbed on with a sponge to reproduce the design on the wave.

Masks: This is the reverse of the stencil. A shape is cut out of paper and laid on the ware; then a sponge dipped in engobe is dabbed around the paper mask.

Spatter: Engobe can be spattered on ware by dipping a stiff bristle brush into the engobe and then drawing a knife blade across the bristles in a direction away from the ware. A different type of spatter can be done with a soft-haired brush. The brush is dipped into the engobe and shaken at the piece.

Sprig decorations are wafer-thin bits of clay formed into decorative shapes and applied to formed leather-hard green ware. This method of decorating was developed by Josiah Wedgwood, who used two colors of clay, usually putting very delicate figures of white clay on a background of colored clay. These shapes are usually made in a sprig mold, which is a block of plaster with a depression shaped like the decorative shape in reverse. To use this mold, a ball of clay smaller than a golf ball is flattened out a bit and pressed into the mold. With a spatula, the clay is trimmed off level with the mold, and then the formed ornament is carefully lifted out of the mold and applied to the leather-hard green ware with slip (Fig. 75).

Designs can be pressed into soft clay with stamps of metal, wood, bisque, or plaster. Stamps may be purchased or made by the ceramist. Impressing can also be done with a roller.

In the wax-resist method the design is painted on the piece with liquid wax, and then the entire surface of the piece is covered with an engobe. The engobe does not adhere to the wax, so the areas painted with wax will remain the original color of the clay piece. During the bisque firing, the wax will burn out and disappear completely. Melted paraffin can be used as the wax, but it must be very hot. It is a little difficult to handle, since it cools rapidly when it touches the surface of the piece. The painting will be much easier if a commercial emulsion of liquid paraffin is used. This can be applied without heating and responds to a brush in much the same manner as tempera paint. It is also much easier on brushes

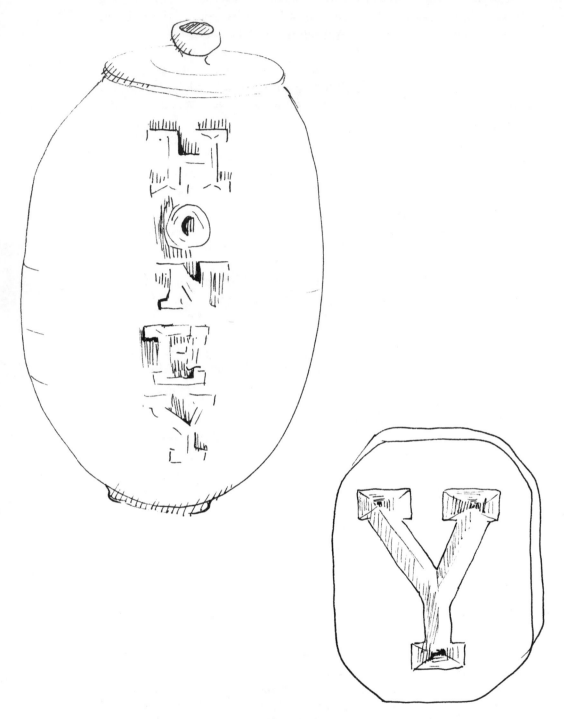

FIG. 75
Sprig decorating

than hot paraffin, which eventually causes the hairs to loosen and fall out. The wax-resist emulsion should be washed out of the brush as soon as possible. If the emulsion hardens in the brush, benzine will be required to remove it.

Underglaze colors are designed to be used on green or bisque ware and then covered with a transparent glaze. The color can be applied with a brush, a sponge, a sprayer, or an airbrush. If a brush is used, three coats are usually needed to obtain good coverage and solid color. The colors change very little in firing, so color combinations and blending can be observed as work progresses. The underglaze dries quickly and can be handled without damage.

DECORATING ON BISQUE

Various colors and effects can be achieved through the use of glazes. Some are transparent; others are opaque. They come commercially prepared in many novelty finishes such as crackle, crystalline, and mat.

Underglaze colors can also be used on bisque (see above).

A recent development offers interesting effects with a crayon of underglaze color. It is used on bisque and leaves a mark much like that left by a wax crayon on paper.

DECORATING ON FIRED GLAZE

Such things as tiles, dinnerware, sculpture, and costume jewelry may be highlighted with overglaze colors. They are water soluble and may be mixed for shading. They are applied either by spraying or by brushing and refiring at cone 018–020.

Gold or platinum color can be penned, brushed, or airbrushed over glaze to highlight and enrich the design. Refiring the piece to cone 019–017 then fuses the metallic material to the glaze.

KILNS

Essentially, a ceramic kiln is an oven which is designed to reach high temperatures, sometimes up to 2,350° F. Most kilns are lined with a refractory material called firebrick and are insulated with dead airspace, fuller's earth, asbestos, glass fiber, or vermiculite to keep the heat in the chamber. Kilns may be heated with wood, oil, gas, or electricity, and they are designed so that the heat will circulate throughout the chamber. There are many types of kilns, homemade and commercial, all with both desirable and undesirable features. The selection of a kiln depends upon the cost of fuel in the area, the type and amount of firing to be done, and the personal preference of the ceramist.

TYPES OF KILNS

A muffle is a chamber made of refractory material in which ceramic pieces are placed for firing. In a muffle kiln (Fig. 76), the flame circulates between the muffle and the outer wall and leaves through the flue at the top. In some muffle kilns, the flames travel in tubes which are inside the muffle. The heat is very evenly distributed in this type of kiln because tubes can be put at the back and at the front of the kiln. There is no danger of the pieces being fired coming in contact with the flame; however, these kilns, which generally use oil or gas for fuel, are expensive to maintain.

There is no muffle in a downdraft kiln (Fig. 77), so the flames come in direct contact with the pieces being fired. This is all right for bisque ware, but glazed pieces must be put into saggers or boxes which act as small muffles. Downdraft kilns are economical to heat, and they will also reach high temperatures. Wood is frequently used to fuel these kilns, which are usually large walk-ins.

Electric kilns are used extensively by groups because they are clean, easy to operate, and safe. They require little space, do not need a flue, and electricity is almost always available. The source of heat is electric elements, which are set into grooves of the refractory brick. The elements may be Nichrome, which can be used for temperatures up to 2,000° F., or Kanthal, which can go as high as 2,300° F. Globar, a carborundum compound in the form of a bar, is used if higher temperatures are required. It requires special

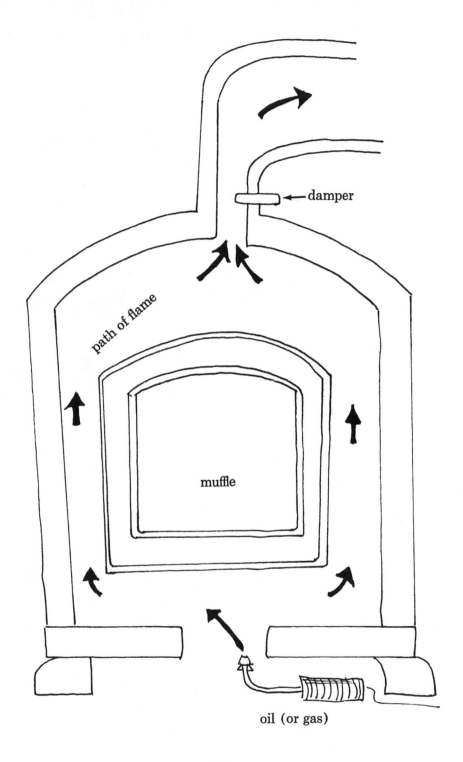

FIG. 76
Portable muffle kiln

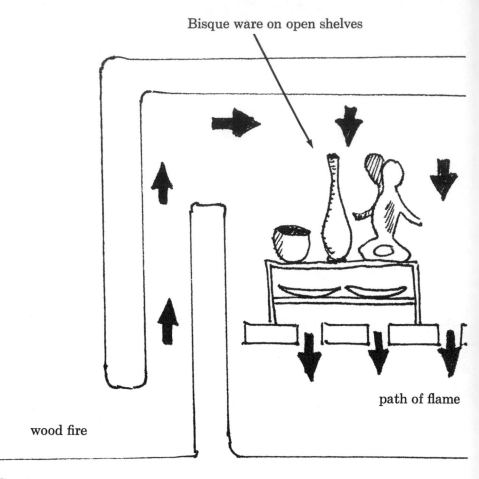

Bisque ware on open shelves

path of flame

wood fire

FIG. 77
Down draft kiln

electrical installation and transformers, but it can be fired up to 2,700° F. Many electric kilns require 220 volts, others use 110 volts, and some models can be ordered with either requirement. The size of electric kilns varies a great deal. If the kiln is small, too much time is required for stacking and unstacking. If it is too large, ceramists must wait too long for a firing. A good-sized kiln for most groups is 16″ × 16″ × 16″ or 18″ × 18″ × 18″. Electric kilns are made to load from the top or from the side. The top-loading kiln is easier to stock, but unlike the side-loading model it cannot be used for enameling. With a top loader, it is important to prop the kiln for cooling so that the props are supported on the metal rather than on the firebrick. When opening and closing a side-loading kiln, care must be taken to keep the firebrick from chipping. The kiln has a

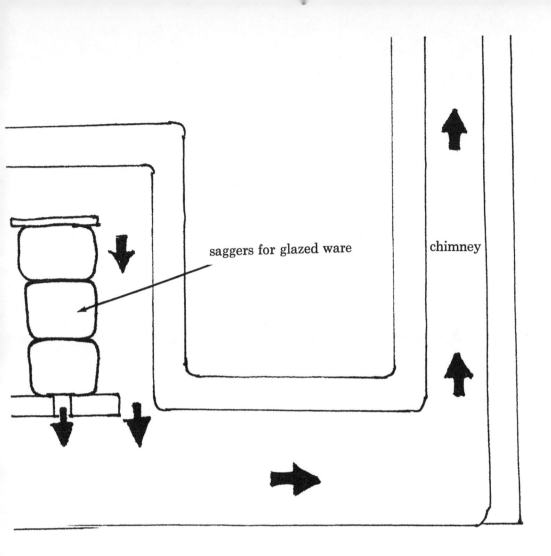

saggers for glazed ware

chimney

peephole which functions as a vapor exhaust in the first stages of firing and as an observation window to check the pyrometric cones in the final stages. In between, the cover may be closed over the hole to prevent loss of heat.

USING THE KILN

Much of the success of good ceramic work depends on skilled firing of the kiln. In order to protect the shelves and floor of the kiln from bits of glaze which may drip, they should be painted with kiln wash at frequent intervals. Kiln wash is a mixture of flint and china clay which does not fuse during firing, so any glaze

FIG. 78
Stacking bisque ware

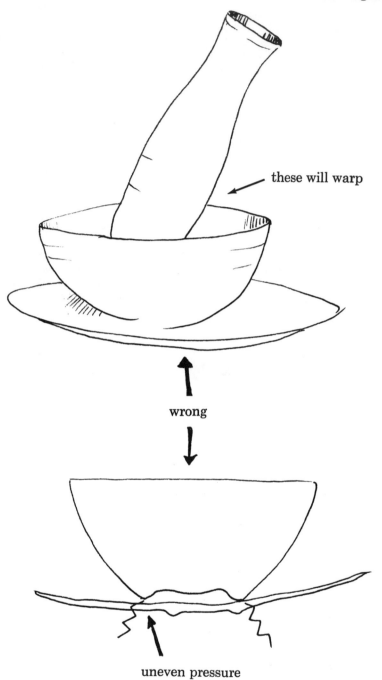

these will warp

wrong

uneven pressure

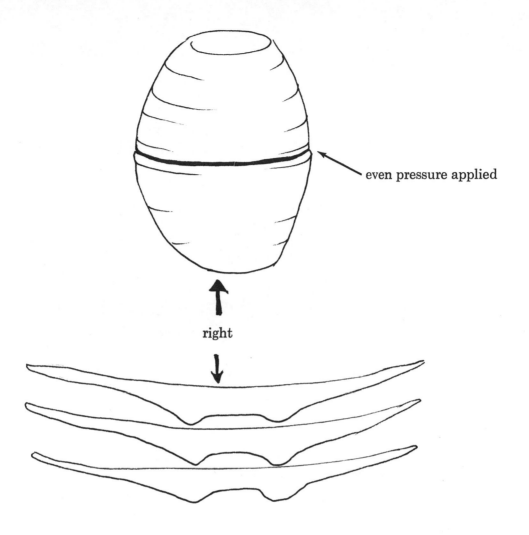

even pressure applied

right

which falls on it can be chipped off. Usually sold in powder form, kiln wash must be mixed with water to the consistency of cream. It is then brushed on the floor and the top surface of the kiln shelves with a varnish brush. *Note:* Do *not* coat the top or the sides of the kiln, or the undersides or edges of the shelves, as the kiln wash may flake off during firing and make ugly blemishes on the glazed pieces.

Stacking the kiln is a real art. First, the pieces must be put in so that they will fire well. Then the kiln should be stacked as full as possible for economy; this will also permit more artists to get their pieces fired sooner. When clay and glaze are purchased, it is usually advisable to select products that fire at the same temperature; then bisque and glaze firing can be done at the same time. Most ceramic companies consider this in the manufacture, but problems may arise if products are bought at several places or if other than

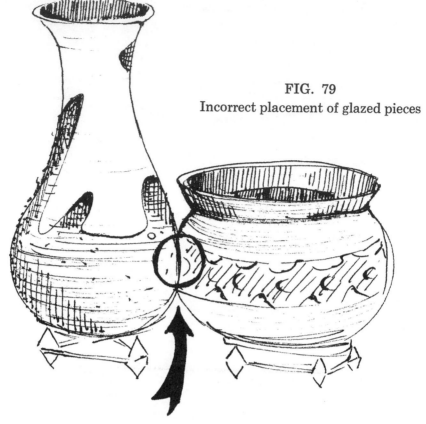

FIG. 79

Incorrect placement of glazed pieces

Wrong! These glazed pieces will fuse

the standard products are bought. Shelf supports, which come in different lengths, are used to support one shelf over the other so that many pieces can be fired at one time.

Unequal pressures on bisque pieces that are being fired tend to warp the pieces because, when clay matures, the fluxes melt and become soft until they are cool again. Unglazed pieces can be stacked close together, even on top of each other, but the distribution of weight on each piece must be kept even (Fig. 78).

Glaze becomes molten when it is fired. During this molten state, a glazed piece will stick permanently to anything it touches (Fig. 79). Because of this, precautions must be taken to prevent sticking.

Glaze should be removed from the base of the foot of the piece. If there is no foot and/or if the base needs to be glazed because the piece is to hold liquid (vases, mugs, etc.), it must be supported up

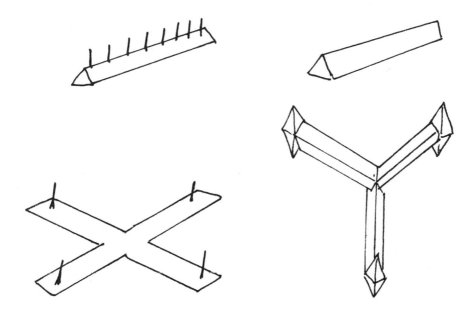

FIG. 80
Types of supports

and off the shelf in some way. There are several types and sizes of supports which can be used for different purposes (Fig. 80). The aim of good stilting is to give adequate support yet have as little of the glazed surface touching the stilt as possible (Fig. 81). If the stilt leaves a rough spot in the glaze, it can be smoothed with a metal file or a grinder. The pieces must be put at least ¼" apart in the kiln and no closer than ¼" from the kiln shelf supports.

The glaze must be sufficiently thick to cover the piece well but not so thick that it will drip. To prevent one piece from dripping on another, the pieces should be placed in such a way that they will drip on a shelf rather than on other pieces. The volatile gases from some glazes have a tendency to tint other glazes in the kiln. So be sure you know which glazes should be fired separately.

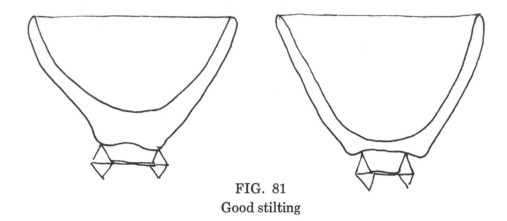

FIG. 81
Good stilting

A person who has stacked the kiln previously does it more easily and can get more into one load than someone with little experience because he has learned some of the following tricks to expedite stacking:

(1) Put pieces of one size on the same shelf so the shelves can be more efficiently packed.

(2) For greater stability of shelves in the kiln, put the flatter pieces at the bottom so the lower shelves do not have to be raised so high.

(3) When a large piece or a piece with a narrow base is stilted, test to see that it is well balanced. Pieces sometimes change shape during firing, causing a top-heavy piece to fall. Such an accident not only spoils the piece that falls, but it frequently rearranges the pieces in the kiln sufficiently to spoil many of them, too.

(4) If there is any danger that a piece might blow up in the kiln, fire it separately.

(5) Be sure that all green ware and glazed pieces are dry before they are put in the kiln. Test them against the cheek. If they feel cool, they are not dry.

(6) Stack during the day, and then leave the kiln open overnight so that the pieces can finish drying.

(7) As the kiln is heating, keep the peephole open to let moisture escape until a cool glazed piece or a mirror held in front of the peephole does not gather condensed moisture.

(8) Stack figurines with the faces pointing away from the elements, which are hotter and may distort the delicate color of the face.

(9) Stack pieces at least 1″ away from the elements.

(10) If the piece is from a mold and the mold does not allow for air holes, put a hole in an inconspicuous place to let the air out.

(11) Be sure that pieces over 1″ thick contain a considerable amount of grog, or make them thinner before firing is attempted.

Even after the piece has been successfully shaped, decorated, and put in the kiln, it is not free from possible damage until after it is fired. Firing must be done with accuracy and patience. The accuracy of the firing depends upon accurate measurement of the temperature within the kiln.

The temperature in the kiln can be measured with pyrometric cones, the most accurate and reliable method; with a kiln sitter, a mechanical type of cutoff which is activated by the bent cone; or with a pyrometer.

Pyrometric cones are slender clay pyramids made with selected fluxes so that they will start to bend at a certain heat. The temperature at which the cone will bend is indicated by a number impressed into one side at the base of the cone. The lower the number, the lower the temperature at which the cone will bend. Table 1 lists cone temperatures, which also indicate the color in the kiln, the effect of that temperature on the clay, and the type of object that should be fired at that temperature. This table is only a general guide. Specific temperature and cone information is on the package of glaze or clay, as well as in the catalog from which it was ordered. Cones are available in two sizes. The larger cones are 2½″ high and have a ½″ base; the smaller ones, which are convenient for small kilns, are 1⅛″ high and have a ¼″ base. The cones are put in a clay pat, positioned so that the number on the cone faces the worker and the cone angles to the right at about 8° from vertical. A series of three cones is recommended for each firing (Fig. 82). The center cone is the firing cone and is selected to bend at the firing temperature of the ware. The warning cone is at the right of the firing cone, positioned so that it will not fall on the other cones. When the warning cone bends, the ceramist knows that the firing cone will bend in a short time. The guard cone indicates whether or not the kiln has been overfired (Fig. 83). The clay pat will explode and cause damage to the ware in the kiln if the clay is not well wedged, if it is too thick and without grog, and if it is put into the kiln before it is completely dry. Cones are put into the kiln *after* it has been stacked. The pat must be placed so that the cones are easily visible through the peephole, yet so that the cone will not touch a piece when it falls. If there are two peepholes, the pat should be placed at the higher one, as the temperature is higher at the top of the kiln. When starting to work with a new kiln, some potters place cone pats at various places to determine the hottest and the coolest spots in order to plan more effective stacking.

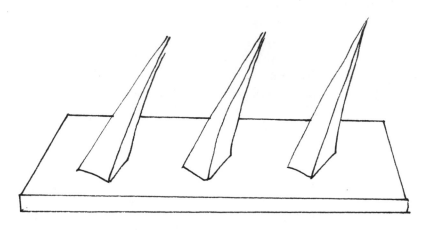

Cone pat set for firing to cone 4

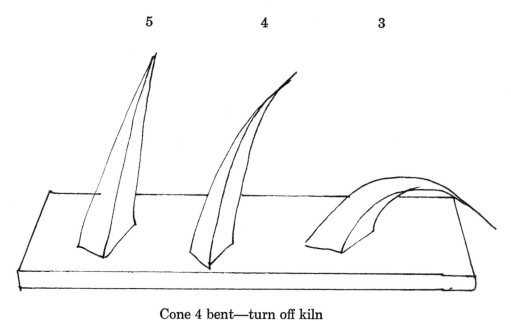

5   4   3

Cone 4 bent—turn off kiln

FIG. 82

Cones set in clay pat for firing

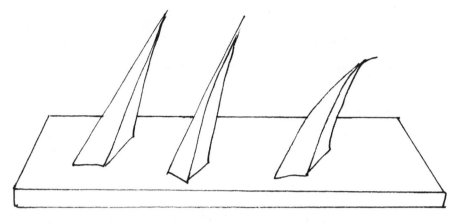

Cone 3 bending—warning signal

5   4   3

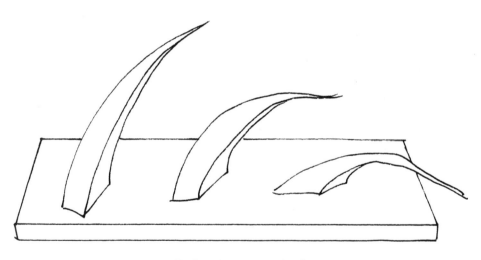

Kiln has been overfired

FIG. 83

TABLE 1.
Cone Temperatures

Cone	Centigrade	Fahrenheit	Color of fire	What happens to clay	Type of ware and glazes
15	1,435	2,615			
14	1,400	2,552			
13	1,350	2,462			
12	1,335	2,435		Porcelain matures	Porcelain
11	1,325	2,417	White		
10	1,305	2,381			
9	1,285	2,345		Stoneware clays	China bodies,
8	1,260	2,300		mature	stoneware,
7	1,250	2,282			salt glazes
6	1,230	2,246			
5	1,205	2,201			
4	1,190	2,174			
3	1,170	2,138		Red clays melt	China glazes
2	1,165	2,129			
1	1,160	2,120			Semivitreous
01	1,145	2,093	Yellow		ware
02	1,125	2,057		Buff clays mature	Earthenware
03	1,115	2,039			
04	1,060	1,940		Red clays mature	
05	1,040	1,904			
06	1,015	1,859			
07	990	1,814			Low-fire
08	950	1,742			earthenware
09	930	1,706	Orange		Low-fire
010	905	1,661			lead glazes
011	895	1,643			
012	875	1,607	Cherry red		Luster glazes
013	860	1,580			
014	830	1,526			
015	805	1,481			
016	795	1,463			
017	770	1,418		Organic matter in	Chrome red
018	720	1,328	Dull red	clay burns out	glazes
019	660	1,220			Overglaze colors
020	650	1,202		Dehydration begins	enamels
021	615	1,139			
022	605	1,121			

A kiln sitter, or kiln guard, is an easily installed mechanical cutoff which is activated when the cone bends. Some of these devices also have timers which can be set to turn off the kiln in the event that the cone does not activate the cutoff. These are quite reliable and inexpensive and are a great help for people who tend to forget the kiln. Because no mechanical device is absolutely foolproof, a kiln should not be fired without pyrometric cones and a responsible person in the area to double check the cutoff mechanism.

Pyrometers are devices which measure the temperature inside the kiln and, if the kiln is electric, cut off the current at the appropriate time. A timer which cuts off the kiln at a certain time is a good precaution to have with the pyrometer. Since the pyrometer is a delicate and expensive piece of equipment which is easily thrown out of adjustment, the kiln should never be left alone when it is being fired, and someone must check to be sure that the kiln has been turned off. Most ceramists use cones with a pyrometer as a double check.

Certain changes in the clay take place as the temperature in the kiln increases. A chart of this cycle in brief is shown in Table 2. To understand these changes is to have better control of what occurs in the kiln.

(1) *Water smoking.* Even though the clay feels dry, it still contains two types of moisture: *atmospheric*, which is from the water in the atmosphere, and *chemically combined water*, which is the water in the molecular structure of the clay particles. In the water-smoking period, the atmospheric water leaves the clay. During this time, before the kiln reaches 300° F., the heat should be raised slowly and a way provided for the moisture to escape. Gas-, oil-, and wood-fired kilns have flues through which moisture escapes. When an electric kiln is fired, the door should be left open a crack during this first period and the peephole should also be left open.

(2) *Complete dehydration.* Before the kiln reaches 1,000° F., the combined water in the clay leaves. The door must be kept closed to get the temperature up this high, but the peephole should be left open until all moisture has escaped.

(3) *Expansion of silica.* At about 1,063° F., the silica in the clay begins to expand; this is a critical period for larger pieces which might expand unevenly and break if firing is too rapid.

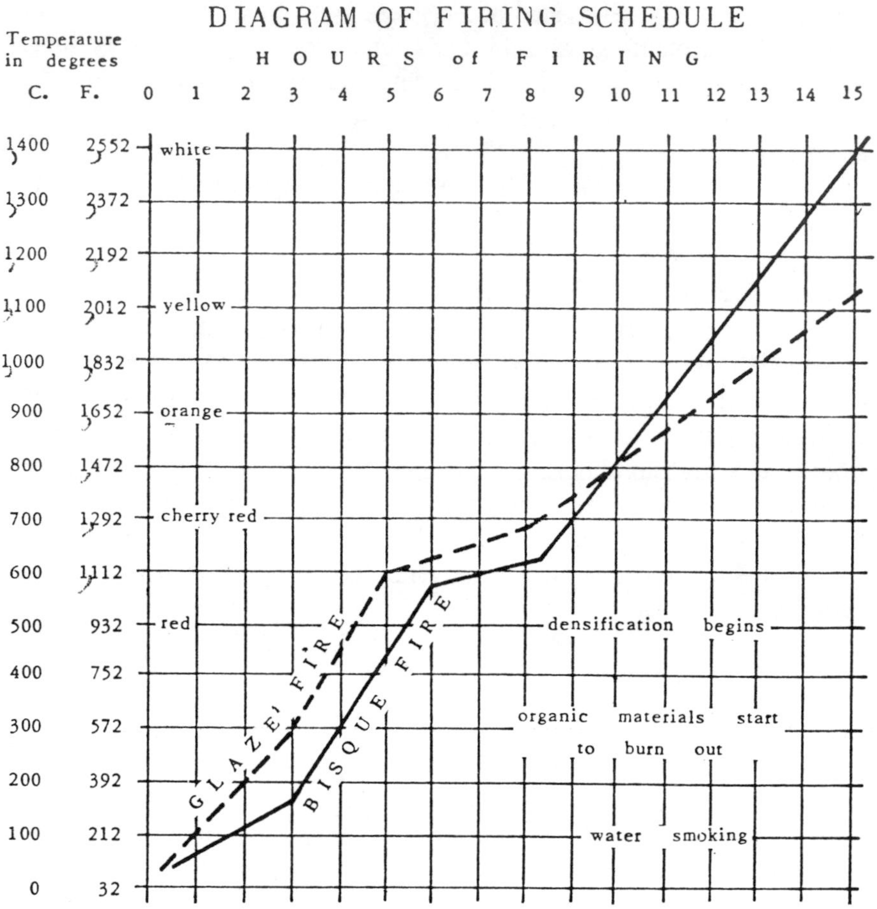

DIAGRAM OF FIRING SCHEDULE

Temperature
in degrees

HOURS of FIRING

| C. | F. | 0 | 1 | 2 | 3 | 4 | 5 | 6 | 7 | 8 | 9 | 10 | 11 | 12 | 13 | 14 | 15 |

1400 — 2552 — white

1300 — 2372

1200 — 2192

1100 — 2012 — yellow

1000 — 1832

900 — 1652 — orange

800 — 1472

700 — 1292 — cherry red

600 — 1112

500 — 932 — red ———— densification begins ————

400 — 752

300 — 572 organic materials start to burn out

200 — 392

100 — 212 water smoking

0 — 32

GLAZE FIRE

BISQUE FIRE

TABLE 2.

Diagram of Firing Schedule

(4) *Burning of organic matter.* Between 1,000° F., and 1,500° F., the organic matter in the clay burns out. If native red clay is being fired, it is important to increase the temperature slowly during this period.

(5) *Color of kiln (cherry red).* At about 1,000° F., the kiln begins to get cherry red and it is possible to see objects inside. This is not true with an electric kiln, in which the elements glow and furnish light before this temperature is reached.

(6) *Firing.* The bending temperature of bisque is reached at 1,121° F. Beyond 1,112° F., the firing of bisque can be speeded up, but glazed pieces must be fired more slowly to prevent the formation of pinholes.

(7) *Maturing of ware.* As soon as the kiln reaches maturing temperature for the clay or glaze being fired, it must be shut off. The damper or the peephole should be left open for about 10 minutes to allow products of combustion to escape.

(8) *Cooling.* The kiln must cool slowly to prevent unwanted crazing and breakage. Any kiln should cool for at least 24 hours. After that time, the cooling may be hastened by opening the door gradually; for example, an inch every half hour as an estimate. This is called cracking the kiln. Do *not* remove pieces from the kiln until they can be removed without the protection of gloves.

MOSAICS

Mosaics

Literature on early mosaics is rather meager, so the origin of the art is not clear. Although the earliest evidence of mosaics is found on jewelry, ivory thrones, and temple columns made in 1400 B.C., it is generally conceded that the art had its beginning as floor decoration. It reached its highest development from 1400–1500 B.C., during which time entire church interiors were decorated in this manner. The art is regaining popularity at present, and the methods employed are basically the same as those that were used in the 1600's. Some contemporary mosaic projects that are practical to make are ash trays, bookends, boxes, coasters, lamp bases, pictures, tabletops, and trivets. Any number of materials may be employed, including ceramic tile (purchased or handmade), cork, glass, paper, pebbles, plastic, rubber or vinyl tile, sand, seeds, shells, and various woods. The use of several of these materials together can result in interesting and often expressive textures.

TOOLS AND EQUIPMENT

BRUSHES. For spreading glue.

MIXING BOWL. For mixing large quantities of grout.

MIXING CUPS. For mixing small quantities of grout. The use of old cans or paper cups will save the time and energy of cleaning containers.

PLASTIC BAGS. For storing materials. Kept this way, material is easy to handle and can be identified without labeling. Cutting tile in the bag offers additional protection from flying chips of tile.

PUTTY KNIFE, TONGUE DEPRESSOR, or RUBBER KIDNEY. For pushing and smoothing grout into the cracks between tiles.

RAGS. For wiping the hands or for wiping grout from the surface of the tiles.

ROLLING PIN. For use with a flathead to level tiles after they are set in place.

SAFETY GLASSES. For protection of the eyes while cutting tile.

SPONGE. For wiping grout from the surface of the tiles.

TILE CUTTERS OR NIPPERS. For cutting small pieces of tile and glass to the desired size and shape. Nippers (Fig. 1) are usually carbide-tipped for extra strength and longevity.

TWEEZERS. For planing the pieces. If the pieces of tile are small or the space into which they fit is small, tweezers facilitate planing.

WOODEN MALLET. For use in combination with a flathead for leveling the tiles after they are set in place (Fig. 2).

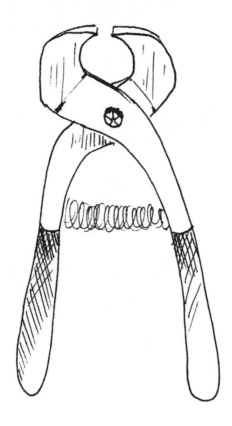

FIG. 1
Tile cutters or nippers

MATERIAL

Glue is used to hold the mosaic material to the background. Casein glue or polyvinyl acetate resin emulsion (Elmer's glue) is commonly used for pieces which will be placed indoors or in any other location where they will not come in contact with water. Epoxy glue is used on pieces which will come in contact with dampness.

Grout is a prepared mixture to which water is added. It is used to fill in the spaces between the mosaic pieces. It can be colored with grout stain to blend with or accent the colors of the mosaic.

Mosaic material can be any one or any combination of the following:

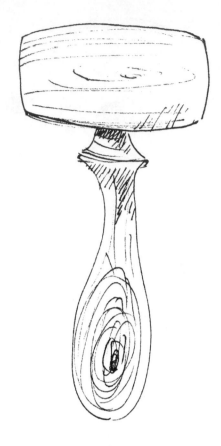

FIG. 2
Wooden mallet

(1) Ceramic tile, which is available in several forms. These can be made from clay and glazed the desired colors. Ready-made tiles are packaged in bags and sold by the pound or fraction of a pound. Some tiles are arranged in a pattern and lightly glued to a coarse netting. These are sold by the sheet (Fig. 3). The sheet is cut to size and then glued to the mounting surface.

(2) Cork, cut and painted.

(3) Glass, crushed or pieces.

(4) Paper.

(5) Pebbles.

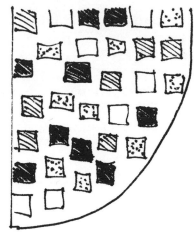

FIG. 3

Various prepatterned ceramic tile sheets

(6) Plastic.

(7) Rubber tiles.

(8) Sand, available in various colors.

(9) Seeds, beans, peas, rice, etc., as well as garden seeds.

(10) Shells.

(11) Vinyl tile.

(12) Woods of different shapes and types. The pieces may be painted or finished to preserve the natural finish.

(13) Wax, silicone, or marble polish to protect the grout.

Mounting surfaces vary according to what is being made. Masonite provides a good base for small projects which will not be in contact with moisture. It is used mainly as a base for pictures up to about 10″× 12″ in size.

Plywood of different thicknesses can be used as a mounting surface for projects *larger* than 10″ × 12″ because it does not bend as readily as Masonite. A consideration, however, with a larger piece is to provide for the weight of the plywood, plus the weight of the tile and grout. The thicknesses of plywood required for various sizes of projects are suggested below.

¼″ plywood for projects 3′ × 3′ or smaller.

½″ plywood for projects 3′ × 6′ or smaller.

¾″ plywood for projects larger than 3′ × 6′.

Both the sides and the edges of plywood can be protected from dampness and any resulting warping by coating them with varnish. If this is done, projects which come in contact with a certain amount of moisture can be made with satisfactory results. The mosaic material must be resistant to water, however, and an epoxylike glue must be used.

Preformed mounting surfaces can be purchased or made.

DESIGN

Simplicity is the keynote to design in this medium. There should be a minimum of color and lines, as too much detail becomes lost in the texture. Strong contrasts of color help to bring out the design. Geometric and free-form designs are especially good for the beginner as he gets the "feel" of the material and tests what can be done with it.

A good way to get an attractive design is to select a motif and repeat it in a variety of ways. Another way is to paint on a large sheet of paper with a brush, using showcard colors. Decorative repetition of geometric designs can be very effective.

PROCEDURES

Results can be highly pleasing and the processes involved are not complex if these steps are followed:

(1) Plan the design and the colors to be used. Paint, crayon,

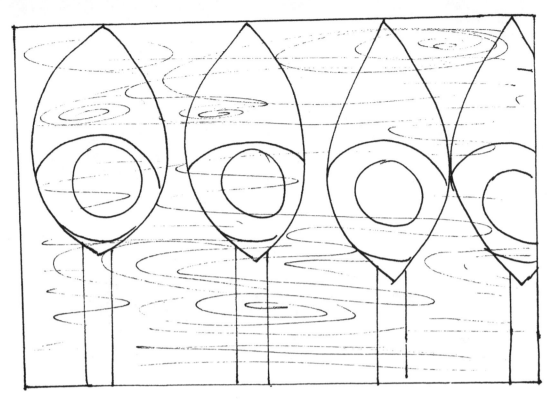

FIG. 4
Design transferred to prepared background

charcoal, cut paper, or even the tiles themselves can be used in the planning.

(2) Transfer the design to the prepared background surface (Fig. 4).

(3) Fit the mosaic pieces into the design. If tiles are used, they may need to be cut with the tile nippers (Fig. 5A) to fit into design shapes (Fig. 5B). Care must be taken to protect the eyes from flying chips of tile by wearing protective glasses or by cutting the tile inside of a plastic bag.

(4) Glue pieces individually or spread glue evenly over an area. The glue should be thick enough to hold the mosaic pieces securely, yet not thick enough to ooze up between the tiles. The size of the area that should be spread with glue depends upon how fast the glue dries, the size of the pieces, and the agility of the worker. The mosaics must be in place before the glue dries. If grout is to be used, the pieces should be set $\frac{1}{16}''$ to $\frac{1}{8}''$ apart to allow space for it.

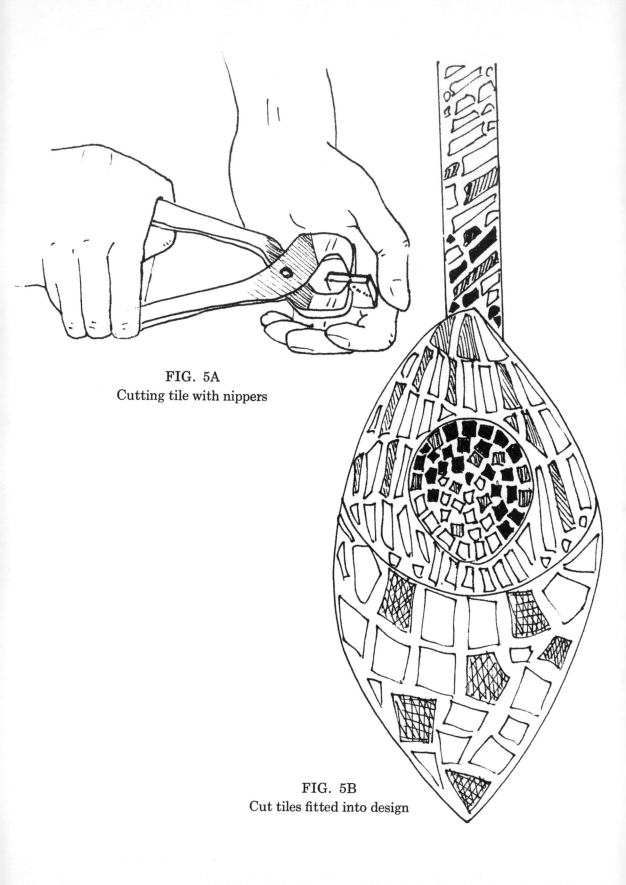

FIG. 5A
Cutting tile with nippers

FIG. 5B
Cut tiles fitted into design

FIG. 6
Pouring the grout

(5) Add grout, if indicated, after the glue is dry. Some types of mosaic materials, such as sand and seeds, do not need grout. However, if grout is used, follow this method: Mix the grout by putting a small amount of water in an appropriate-sized container and adding the powdered grout until it is the consistency of heavy cream. If the mosaic is vertical or if it is not framed, make the grout thicker. Pour and spread the grout over the surface (Fig. 6) and rub it into the spaces between the tiles with the hand, a tongue depressor, or a rubber kidney. Allow time for the grout to set; then remove it from the surface of the tiles with a dampened sponge, rag, or paper towel.

(6) Give the surface a final cleaning (Fig. 7) to ensure that all grout is removed. When the grout is completely dry, apply silicone, marble polish, or wax to protect it.

Note: If tile is purchased by the sheet, cut the sheet to size and start with Step 4 above. To fill all areas with tile, some of the tiles may need to be pulled from the netting, cut, and fitted into the empty space.

FIG. 7
Spreading and removing excess grout

SAFETY

Making mosaics is not dangerous. Safety glasses, cutting the tile in plastic bags, and any other suggestions in this chapter should be followed, however, when handling and cutting the tiles.

STAINED GLASS

BY JOE CASTAGNA

Stained Glass

Glass was first created during the early days of the earth when volcanoes combined sand and ashes with intense heat to form obsidian. Other forms of glass, including quartz, amethyst, onyx, and agate, were also created under similar conditions.

The discovery of glass making seems to have been somewhat accidental, and its actual production can be traced back to 4000 B.C. in northeast Africa, mainly in Syria and Egypt.

Glass is composed of silica sand, soda ash, and limestone, with traces of borax and iron. The mixture is finely sifted and heated to 2,500° F. (1,400° C.). Certain metal oxides and salts added to the mixture give the glass its color. The following list shows the colors and the metals used to produce them:

Red   selenium, cadmium salt, gold oxide, copper salts

Orange selenium, copper salts

Yellow selenium, chromium salts, cadmium sulfide, sodium,

Blue   cobalt, chromium salts, copper salts

Purple manganese with cobalt

Black   concentrated copper salts

Green   copper salts, chromium salts, and iron oxide.

To produce opalescent colors, either fluorides or soda ash are introduced into the mixture, giving the glass its opaque, milky quality.

Molten glass may be worked in many ways. The fastest and most economical is to pour the glass onto a metal bed and then pass it through steel rollers. The rollers can be smooth, creating what's known as the double-roll texture, or they can be patterned. Different kinds of patterned textures available are hammered, granite, and flemish—the most popular. The glass produced by this machine-made process is called cathedral glass. This is the most common type of glass and is easily recognized by its uniform thickness, texture, and pattern. Cathedral glass is almost always transparent, easy to cut, and inexpensive.

Opalescent glass is basically cathedral glass with fluoride or soda ash added to give it an opaque quality. Patterns such as double roll, granite, and hammer are also embossed on opals. Opalescents are almost never transparent, making them perfectly suited for use in lamps or lamp shades. They are generally more difficult to cut than other varieties of glass, and the best results are obtained with a carbide cutter.

A recent innovation in glass manufacturing has been the creation of hand-rolled glass. Instead of passing through machine rollers, the glass is manually rolled to give it a nonuniform texture and quality reminiscent of Tiffany's own glass. This glass is usually referred to as cat's paw glass (because of the pattern, which resembles little cat's paw prints). It is relatively easy to cut and comes in almost unlimited color combinations, mainly opalescent-based.

The most exciting variety of glass is antique glass. The term "antique" refers to the process used in making the glass, not to the age of the glass. This glass is hand-blown, and its uneven thickness, seeds, bubbles, seams, streaks, and countless other irregularities give it an unsurpassed beauty. Antique glass is easy to cut and comes in thousands of hues and color tones. This glass is produced by one firm in the United States, Blenko in West Virginia. Most of it comes from England, France, and Germany, where skilled artisans still produce it with blowpipes. The blowpipe is credited to the ancient Syrians, circa 3500 B.C., and has remained virtually unchanged up to the present day. Antique glass is used to create beautiful vases, bowls, lamp shades, and many other decorative pieces.

Transparent glass was first introduced around 550 B.C. Very little was done with glass for almost a millennium, but around the year A.D. 500, churches started using glass for their windows. At this time, glass was still prized more for its decorative value than for its functionality, but as more countries began producing glass, many uses were found for this unique substance. Up until the 12th century, the creation of stained-glass church windows grew into a renowned art form. Then the church itself put a ban on the richly colored windows, and for roughly 100 years it stopped developing them. Around A.D. 1270 the art was welcomed back for almost a century until the church again ordered the cessation of all stained-glass work. Caught in a web of religious and political *bouffonerie*, the art of stained glass slept for another few hundred years. Some interest was rekindled during the 1700's, mainly because glass became plentiful and affordable.

The real surge in glass art came at the start of the 20th century. Louis C. Tiffany was very instrumental in reviving the art form and making it more accessible to the public for private use. However, the appreciation of stained glass and its role in the progressive art movement again declined until fairly recently.

Few things surpass the beauty of a well-executed stained-glass work—especially if you've created the piece yourself. The joy of working with glass and the beauty of the final results have aroused increasing interest within the art world. As a medium, stained glass has been in use as a spiritual reflection and a source of enlightenment by many religions since the beginning of civilization. We are now experiencing a glass renaissance, a newly revived interest in an age-old art combining ancient and modern methods and materials and covering every art form, both classical and abstract. An increasing number of people are embellishing their homes with beautiful stained-glass windows, lamp shades, and other decorative objects.

GLOSSARY

Annealing. The gradual cooling of glass to reduce its brittleness and increase its toughness.

Antique glass. A very transparent glass made by the medieval hand-blown method. Distinguished by its irregular surface texture and thickness, its character and beauty lie in the seeds, bubbles, and flow of varying hues of color within a sheet.

Antiquing solution. A mixture of hydrochloric acid and a wetting agent which produces a dark gray-to-black finish when applied to the surface of lead or solder.

Backlighting. The most effective way to display decorative glass.

Beading. A buildup of lead on the solder line, which produces a smooth, rounded ridge and gives the design added character. To produce beading, it's important to keep iron temperature at a controlled, lower temperature.

Bench brush. A tool used to remove small glass splinters from the work surface.

Blenko glass. The only American hand-blown glass, distinguished by an even greater variation in thickness within a sheet than the European hand-blown glass.

Brass channels. Strips of U-shaped brass came used for finishing and lamps.

Breaking pliers. Flat-nosed, smooth 6″ pliers, used to snap off glass pieces too small to be broken by hand. Jaw widths available are 9/16″ and 1″ flare (the 9/16″ is preferred for stained-glass work).

Bubbles. A texture found within antique glass. It is formed when the blowpipe is withdrawn before the mixture of silica, sand, borax, and color material has boiled itself free of sulfurous gases.

Burnisher. A wooden stick used to smooth copper foil down to glass.

Carbide cutter. A glass cutter with a tungsten carbide wheel, used to cut opalescent glass.

Carborundum stone. A tool used to remove sharp edges and nubs from glass.

Cathedral glass. Domestic, machine-rolled glass with a heavy, regular texture impressed on one side by mechanical rollers. Available in a variety of textures, including hammer, flemish, ripple, and granite.

Cartoon. A full-size drawing of a design layout.

Circle cutter. A cutting wheel attached to a gauged arm which moves around a central hub.

Copper foil. Adhesive-backed and available in a variety of widths, the most popular sizes being $3/16''$, $7/32''$, and $1/4''$. Foil is used when the glass pieces are small and for three-dimensional work.

Crackle glass. Antique glass dipped in water immediately after it is formed, producing a fractured effect.

Cut line. The tracing of the cartoon lead lines on heavy paper.

Dalle-de-verre. A French term for slab glass first produced by the French in the 1930's. The glass chunks are approximately $8'' \times 12''$, and range in thickness from $3/4''$ to $1\frac{1}{4}''$.

Etching. Using hydrofluoric acid to eat away the thin top layer of flash glass, exposing its base color.

Faceting. Chipping of slab glass.

Flash glass. A form of antique glass consisting of a thick base layer of color and then coated with a second thin layer of a different color.

Flux. This material is applied to the metal before the solder is put on. It helps the solder run smoothly, cleans the metal, and prevents oxidation of the solder, promoting adhesion of the two metals. The most popular flux is oleic acid.

Flux brush. An acid-resisting brush used to apply flux to areas being soldered.

Fusing. The adhesion of one piece of glass to another by heating at high temperatures in a kiln.

Glass. A hard, amorphous, brittle, transparent substance made by fusing one or more of the silicon oxides, boron, or phosphorus with certain basic oxides.

Glass cutter. A tool used to score glass so it can be broken into specific shapes. It has a steel or tungsten carbide wheel rotating on an axle with a wood or metal handle.

Glass scriber. A pencil-like instrument with a carbide or diamond tip, used for writing or etching on glass.

Glazing. Fitting, assembling, and positioning pieces of glass and lead together.

Glazing board. A work surface composed of plywood or homosote and larger than the panel with ½″ thick by 1½″ wide wood strips the length of the panel placed at right angles to one another along two edges.

Glazing knife. See *Lead knife.*

Glazing nails. Tapered nails used to hold glass and lead in position; also referred to as horseshoe nails.

Grozing. The process by which unwanted rough edges are chipped off the cut glass a little at a time.

Grozing pliers. Pliers made of soft metal, usually having narrow, serrated jaws, used to shape glass.

Gum arabic. Used in glass paints to make them adhere to the glass.

Heart. The center part of the lead came.

Homosote. Fire-retardant ½″-thick pressed board; an excellent work surface.

Iron clad tips. Soldering iron tips with a copper core and iron coating; they perform much better than copper tips.

Jewels. Small, decorative pressed glass pieces having flat bottoms and raised tops; available in a wide range of sizes, colors, and shapes, including multifaceted and pyramid forms.

Kiln. A furnace where glass is fired.

Lathekin. A wood tool used to open the channel of lead came.

Lead came. Grooved strips of lead used to hold glass together.

Leading up. Assembling pieces of glass in a stained-glass panel by using lead came.

Lead knife. A double-edged knife, usually having a curved edge, used for cutting lead came.

Lead vise. Used for stretching lead came to give the lead more body and remove the bends; boat cleats work well as lead vises.

Leaves. The surface, measured sides of lead came.

Miter joints. Points where lead intersects and ends are cut and beveled at equal angles.

Muff. The glass cylinder produced when blowing antique glass.

Oleic acid. A natural fatty flux used mainly for lead work.

Opalescent glass. The transmission of light through this glass is greatly reduced but not totally eliminated, allowing for even diffusion of light. It always consists of more than one color, and the subtle effect it produces is best suited for lamp making.

Patina. An antiquing solution of copper sulfate which turns the solder a copper color, giving the piece an aged look; it is applied after the piece has been cleaned.

Pattern knife. A double-bladed utility knife with a shim between the blades.

Pattern paper. Oaktag paper used to guide glass cutter.

Pattern scissors. These special scissors have a double bottom blade for removing the necessary material from pattern pieces to accommodate the lead came.

Pot glass. An antique, hand-blown glass, made by using one pot of color. (A pot is the vat where molten glass is kept in flux while the antique glass is being blown.)

Putty. Used to seal, weatherproof, and strengthen lead panels.

Reamy glass. A hand-blown glass with one or more colors applied in a swirling pattern; more transparent and easier to cut than streaky glass.

Rondel. Circular-shaped glass either hand-spun or machine-pressed. Comes in all sizes and colors and in different textures and patterns; rounded edges make it easy to work with. A characteristic of the hand-blown rondel is the snapped-off mark in its center. Machine-pressed centers are smooth.

Run. Used to describe what happens to a score when you start to break the piece and it penetrates the entire thickness of the glass.

Running pliers. Used to run a score line to produce a clean break.

Safety glasses. Used mainly to protect eyes from splintering glass; lightly tinted sunglasses or plain glasses are suitable.

Score. A controlled cutting process on glass.

Scrub brush. Used to apply putty.

Seeds. Tiny bubbles found in antique glass, one of its distinct characteristics.

Solder. An alloy of tin and lead; the preferred solder in stained-glass work is 60/40. The percentage of tin always precedes the lead.

Soldering. The joining of two metals.

Soldering iron. An electrical tool used to melt the solder.

Sponge. Used to clean the soldering iron tip.

Stopping knife. A glazing tool featuring a flat, rounded blade, used to fit the glass properly in the lead came channels.

Straightedge. Metal or wood rulers used for straight-line cutting and measuring.

Streaky glass. A hand-blown glass of more than one color streaked across its surface. Unlike the opalescents, it is transparent; each sheet is a work of art in itself and should not be cut into smaller pieces.

Support bars. Usually made of galvanized steel and used to support panels larger than 4 square feet.

Ties. Copper wire strips soldered to a panel, enabling it to be attached to support bars.

Tinned wire. Copper wire with a tin coating, used to make hooks and to provide extra support for small projects.

Tinning. The application of a thin coat of solder to the copper tip of the soldering iron. In copper foil work, tinning refers to the coating of all copper surfaces with solder.

Tungsten carbide. The hardest metal, used for the wheels on glass cutters.

Whiting. Powdered calcium carbonate, a cleaning compound, used to polish pieces.

Wire brush. Used to clean lead joints and remove stubborn oxidation, thereby improving the solder joint.

Zinc chloride. A strong chemical flux used for copper foil work.

GLASS CUTTING

The uninitiated have many misconceptions about what glass cutting actually entails. The following in-depth information should not only remove any myths about glass cutting but should also prove to be invaluable in developing an understanding of the process.

In essence, a glass cutter is a very small sharp wheel with a handle (Fig. 1). The cutting wheel does not *cut*, but *scores* the glass to create a minute fracture. The wheel is drawn across the smooth surface of the glass with a moderate amount of pressure, similar to the pressure one would put on a pencil when making a carbon copy. This uniform pressure creates a fracture line which penetrates the glass. When pressure is applied to both sides of this line, the glass will break along the fracture (path of least resistance). The cutter should always be held with the handle between the index and middle fingers, supported from behind by the thumb (Figs. 2A and 2B). This position offers the greatest amount of mobility and control.

Most cutters incorporate a metal or wood handle with a steel wheel, while the better cutters are made of tungsten carbide, the hardest man-made material. Steel-wheel cutters are also good, and for some types of glass they are preferred. Good cutting will result in a better quality of craftsmanship in the finished piece. Glass cutters are available with different size wheels and bevel angles, and each wheel serves a different function. Although some wheel sizes are designated as general all-purpose cutters, it is best to use a cutter designed for the specific kind of cutting to be done.

Most cutters are numerically sized; steel wheels are usually color-coded as to size, while carbides are number-stamped. The larger the number, the smaller the wheel. The range is generally 1–9, with 1 being the largest wheel and 9 the smallest. Cutters with a ball end for tapping are best for beginners. Small-wheel

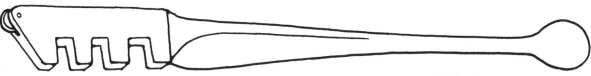

FIG. 1
Glass cutter.

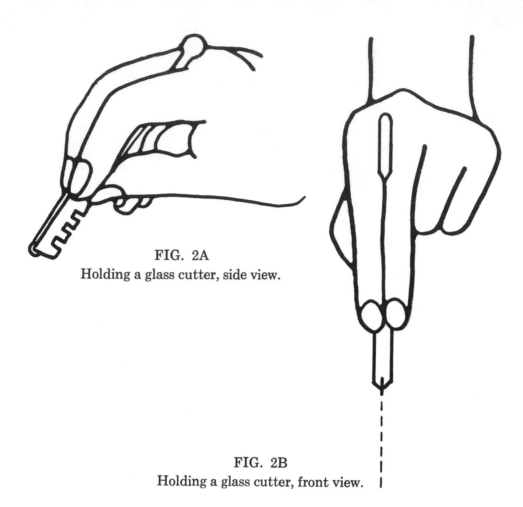

FIG. 2A
Holding a glass cutter, side view.

FIG. 2B
Holding a glass cutter, front view.

cutters work well for pattern cutting and intricate cuts, while their larger-wheeled counterparts are best for straight-line cutting. When working with glass cutters, always keep them in kerosene. If you must store them elsewhere, apply a light oil to the wheel and axle. Aside from lubricating and protecting the cutter, the kerosene will seep into the fracture, allowing for easier separation of the glass.

CUTTING LINES

Straight-line cutting is the easiest type of cut. Make sure the glass surface is clean; soiled or dirty glass surfaces will result in a bad cut and may damage the cutting wheel. Hold your glass cut-

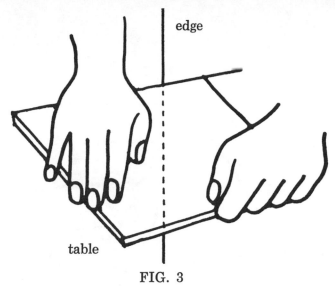

edge

table

FIG. 3

Separating two pieces of glass using a table edge.

ter correctly and dip it in kerosene. Additional kerosene may be applied directly onto the glass surface along the path of the line to be scored. This application of kerosene will limit flaking and chipping and will improve the break-out. Starting at the edge farthest from you, place the whccl as near the edge as possible. At this point, start drawing the cutter toward you with a uniform pressure, just shy of creating any chipping or splintering of the surface. To obtain a good cut, continue your score line right off the edge of the glass. Once you run your score line, don't go over any part of it, or you will destroy the fracture, create an undesirable furrow, and possibly damage the wheel. The glass should be scored only one time, forcefully enough to create a good fracture without leaving a gritty score line. The score line should be barely visible under the reflected light. Remember, a single uniform cut line will develop the correct fracture. The speed with which the cutter is drawn over the glass varies with the type of cutting being done. Although faster speeds are recommended for straight-line cutting, good results can be achieved by using a slower speed on curves or intricate patterns. Whatever speed you choose, it is important to keep it constant over the entire length of the cut. In other words, don't vary your speed in the middle of a cut or you will produce an uneven fracture resulting in an unsatisfactory edge.

Once the score has been created, the separation, or break-out, must be done as soon as possible because glass will restructure itself and the fracture line will become nothing but a scratch on the surface. When separating large pieces of glass, several methods may be employed. The first is to line up the score parallel with the table edge, with the score line just inside the edge (Fig. 3).

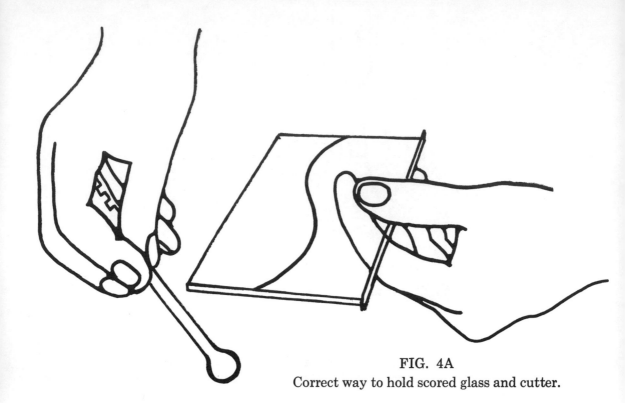

Exert a firm downward pressure, and the pieces should separate easily. If not, slide the sheet back onto the table. (*Note:* Never leave a scored sheet of glass hanging off a table or tap a score without some means of support because the weight of the glass overhang may be enough to cause a hazardous situation.) When tapping large pieces of glass, extend the sheet off the table a few inches with the score perpendicular to the table edge. To initiate the run, it is best to use the ball end of your cutter. Copper or hard plastic round tappers are preferred because they prevent scaling or chipping of the glass edge. With the tapper in hand, tap the glass directly under the score line with a firm upward blow (Figs. 4A and 4B). Tap within an inch of the edge in order to extend the fracture through the entire thickness of the glass sheet. If the cut is a long one, you may want to tap the other side of the score as well. After the run has been produced, it should be visible when looking at the score line from an angle on either side. Hold one of the pieces to be separated with both hands, one on each of the outside edges, and pull the sheet around until you line up the score with the table edge. Don't lift the glass too much while positioning it or it may crack prematurely. Keep the sheet as flat as possible while shifting it around. Now that the glass is in place, apply a uniform and moderate downward pres-

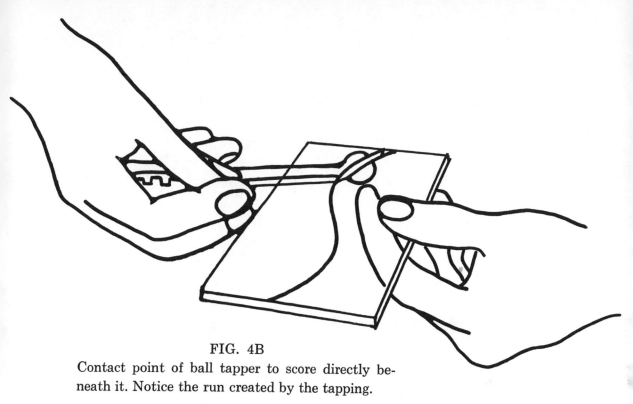

FIG. 4B

Contact point of ball tapper to score directly beneath it. Notice the run created by the tapping.

sure with both hands. The glass should separate quite easily at
this point.

When working with pieces of glass smaller than a square foot,
grip both sides at a point close to the score line (Fig. 5). With
a moderate amount of pressure exerted under and away from the
score, the pieces should come apart easily. The motion involved
here is almost like a bending or folding. Breaking can also be accomplished by placing a cutter handle, pencil, wooden matchstick,
or ruler directly under one edge of the score line and applying
pressure on both sides.

When cutting thin, narrow strips, use the breaking pliers to
get a clean, safe break.

CUTTING CIRCLES

In order to cut clean, uniform circles, it is best to use a circle
cutter. A few varieties are available: one is similar to a compass,
consisting of a suction cup and an adjustable wheel head on a
long arm permanently connected at one end to the suction cup
hub (Fig. 6).

Determine the size of the circle to be cut, and then adjust the

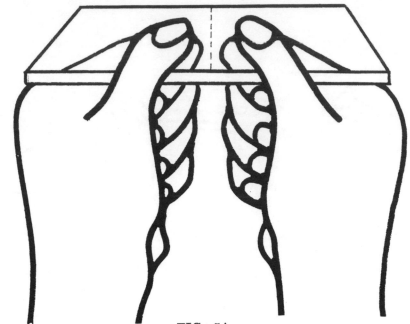

FIG. 5A

Correct way to hold scored piece of glass before the break.

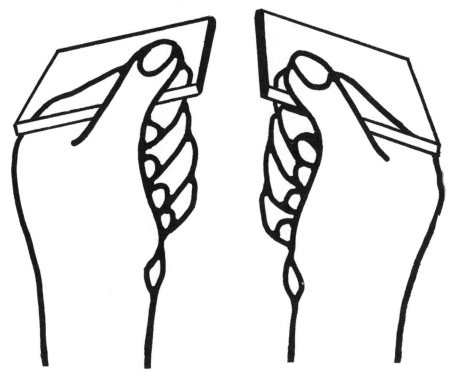

FIG. 5B

Correct position of hands after the break.

FIG. 6
Circle cutter.

wheel head along the ruled arm until you obtain the desired diameter. Apply kerosene to the wheel and to the glass surface along the circumference of the circle.

Place the glass on a firm, flat surface—preferably indoor-outdoor carpet. Tight-napped carpet or a thick pad of newspapers make good substitutes.

Now place the suction cup on the area which will be the center point of the circle. Make sure you have a clearance on all sides of the circle of *at least* 1″ from the edge of the sheet.

While pressing down firmly on the suction cup with one thumb, steadily press the wheel head with the other hand, moving the cutting wheel much as you would a compass. It's best to practice swinging the cutter a full 360° on a soft surface to determine which position to start with in order to obtain *one* continuous and uniform score line. Keep the pressure even, don't go over the score a second time, and be careful not to shift the suction cup hub during this process or you will distort the circle. If the cut is not uniform or continuous, it is best to try another piece of glass.

There are two ways to break out the circle. The first is to tap the score line from underneath with the ball end of your cutter or tapper while holding the glass sheet. Watch carefully for the run to develop, and continue tapping until the run is completely around the circle. The circle is separated at this point, but in order to remove it, a series of tangent lines must be cut from the circle to an outside edge of the sheet of glass (Fig. 7). You can break off the pieces by hand or with the breaking pliers, or tap the tangent lines and remove the excess pieces of glass from around the circle. Some grozing may have to be done to remove any rough pieces, chips, or scales still attached to the circle.

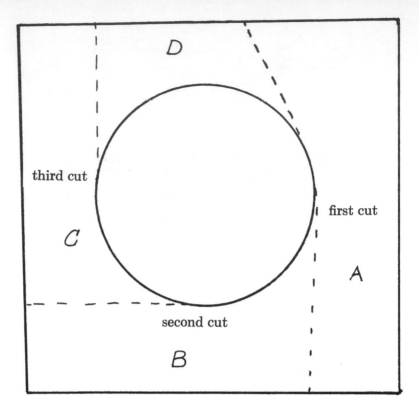

FIG. 7

Breaking out a circle using tangent cuts. After creating a run around the entire circumference of the circle, make cut 1 and break off section A. Make cut 2 and break off B. Then make cut 3 and remove section C. D should fall off by itself, leaving you with a clean, smooth circle.

The second method used to break out the circle is as follows: Make your cut as described, but instead of tapping, turn the sheet of glass over on a piece of indoor-outdoor carpeting, homosote board, or corrugated cardboard. Apply enough pressure with your thumb to start a run in the glass. Continue the run completely around the circle edge by applying pressure directly behind the run until it penetrates the glass around the entire outer edge of the circle. Again, make a few tangent scores from the circle to the edge of the glass sheet and break off the pieces one by one. This method usually produces a better, cleaner-edged circle.

If you are interested in making circles no larger than 5″, a lens cutter (Fig. 8) is an excellent tool. It works pretty much like the previously mentioned cutter except the cutting arm is mounted on a permanent stand. No suction cup is used, and a more precise circle can be cut. Once cut, the circle is broken out as described above.

CUTTING CURVES AND UNUSUAL SHAPES

When cutting slight curves, it is best to try to break the piece out by hand or with a light tap on either end of the score line. Sharp curves require different techniques. In Figs. 9A and 9B you see the cuts necessary to remove the desired pieces of glass: Line 1 should be cut and the complete break made; then lines 2 and 3 should each be cut and broken off. Starting at the center of the curve, tap the complete score line and then the tangent lines, which will result in an easier break-out and cleaner edge.

When cutting sharp angles it is necessary to round them off or the cut will be virtually impossible to make. Right angles are very difficult and should be attempted only after a fair amount of cutting skill has been acquired. When cutting odd shapes, try to take advantage of any lines which might already be available on the glass sheet to be used, or try to determine how best to use the glass with a minimum amount of waste (Figs. 10A, 10B).

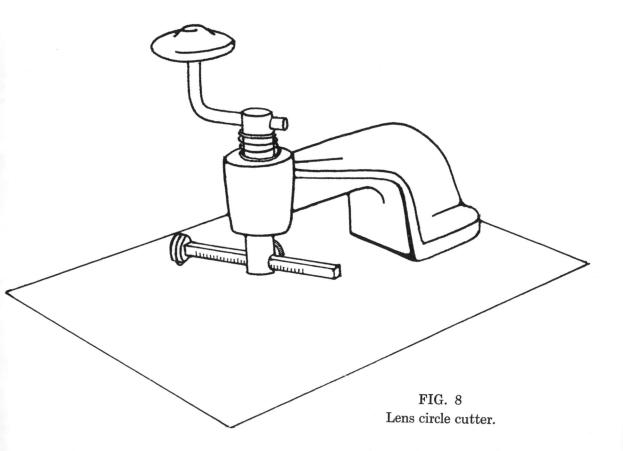

FIG. 8
Lens circle cutter.

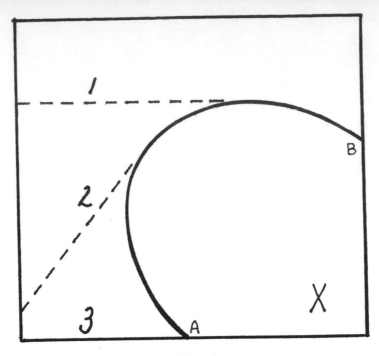

FIG. 9A

To cut section X, make the complete cut AB and than tap, creating a run from points A to B. Then make cut 1 and remove. Make cut 2 and remove that section. At this point, section 3 should fall out or be removed easily with a little pressure.

FIG. 9B

In order to cut section Y, make the desired cut CD and tap. Then make cut 1, break off that section, make a series of congruent cuts to the edge, and tap. Whatever doesn't break out is removed with breaking pliers.

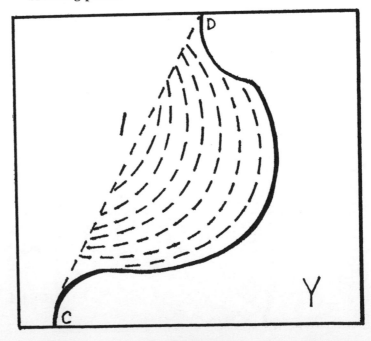

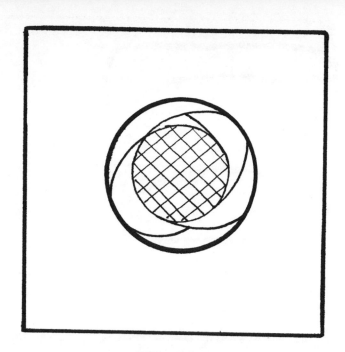

FIG. 10A

To make a round hole in a piece of glass. After scoring and tapping the desired circular cut, score a smaller circle within the area to be removed and tap. Make a series of crisscross score lines in the center along with a few tangent cuts between the two circular cuts. Starting in the middle of crisscross score lines, tap until runs appear in the entire center portion of the area to be removed. The pieces of glass will start to fall out by themselves after sufficient tapping. Don't be impatient and tap too hard, or you'll lose the entire piece.

FIG. 10B

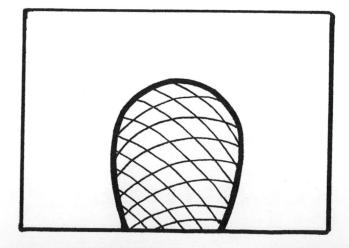

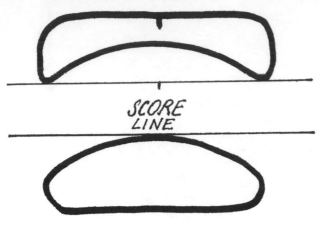

FIG. 11A

Running pliers (frontal view) lined up with score line (note notch in upper jaw of plier).

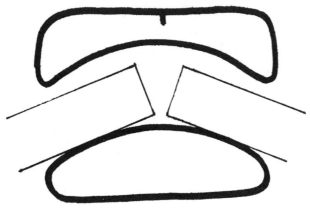

FIG. 11B

How glass separated after slight pressure was applied. Using less pressure, a run could be initiated without the separation of the pieces.

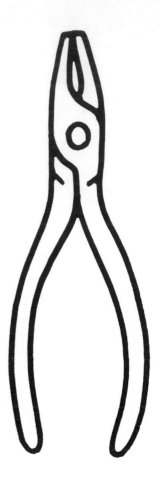

FIG. 12
Breaking pliers.

TOOLS

The running plier is an excellent tool for helping to break out curved or straight cuts. This implement features two curved matching jaws; when the line on the upper jaw is matched with the score line and a little pressure is applied on the handle, a run will develop (Figs. 11A, 11B). If the score line contains a few curves, or if it's a very long one, repeat the process on the other end of the score. Separate the pieces with your hands or breakers for a nice, smooth, uniform cut.

When working with very small pieces of glass, you will find it extremely difficult to separate the pieces with your hands. In

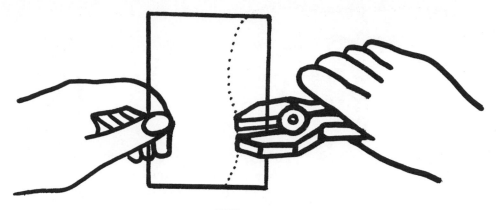

FIG. 13A

Position of the breaking pliers in relation to the scored glass.

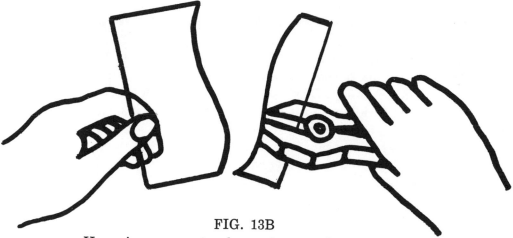

FIG. 13B

How pieces separate when a downward pressure is applied to the pliers.

order to do this properly, use breaking pliers (Fig. 12) which offer better grip and leverage. To use the breaking pliers effectively, it is best to grip the glass with the pliers on one side of the score line, holding the other side in your hand or flat on a table with the score line hanging over the edge. Hold the pliers firmly within an inch of one of the ends but just a hairline away from the score so that the score is visible. At the same time, make a quick, bending motion (down and out) with the pliers, and the pieces will separate easily (Figs. 13A, 13B). The breaking pliers can also be used to start a run by slowly moving them until you hear the run start, then moving to the other end of the score line and repeating the process to make one clean, continuous break. This is especially effective when a long, thin strip is desired.

GROZING

The cutting process is followed by grozing and shaping. Grozing refers to the reshaping of a rough cut, a miscalculated cut, or a very intricate cut to correspond to the pattern. Grozing is best done with grozing pliers, which are composed of soft metal and make it possible to chip the glass, rather than fracture it as regular metal pliers would.

GROZIERS

Grozing pliers come in many shapes and serve different purposes. The most widely used pliers are medium-sized, flat-jawed groziers (Fig. 14). The jaws are approximately 1½" long and about 9/16" wide with little teeth. The plier itself measures about 6". These pliers are best for removing flared edges or reshaping outside corners or curves.

There is also a smaller version of the same pliers, which is excellent for working with small, delicate pieces. Then there are the pincher-type groziers, also known as tongs, which are useful for inside cuts and fine work where little glass is to be removed. These pliers are generally larger than any of the other groziers, but the biting surface is very small to ensure good control and the ability to groze out inner cuts (Fig. 15). There are also curved-nose groziers, which have one regular and one curved jaw to allow the pliers to do almost any grozing job well, and round-nosed groziers, used for inside cuts and for smoothing off edges without chipping.

FIG. 14
Grozing pliers.

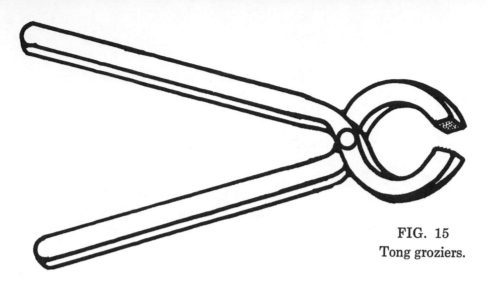

FIG. 15
Tong groziers.

Groziers come in many other sizes and shapes, but these are the most widely used and are the basis for most of the other types. Groziers should be used when a cut has not responded properly and leaves a rough edge or has irregularities which must be removed. The grozier is also used to chew the unwanted small pieces of glass left hanging onto the piece of glass being cut. The chewing motion of the groziers offers more control and a better grozing job when only the inside edge of the jaws is used.

SANDERS

A portable hand sander is very good for cleaning glass edges and smoothing them down. Use a 60-grit silicon-carbide belt for coarse sanding, and a 220 for fine work. Don't keep the belt on the glass during the procedure or overheating will occur. As you work, move the sander back and forth across the surface being finished and lift it off the work entirely several times while grinding. (*Note:* Whether grozing or grinding, remember to wear safety glasses since this is the most hazardous area involved in glass working.) When working with hand sanders, it is best to apply a light oil to the edges being ground to cut down on the amount of glass dust produced. Invest in a surgical mask or some type of filter to keep from breathing tiny glass particles into the lungs.

Carborundum stones or paper can also be used to grind away certain types of unwanted nubs and ridges, and the ultimate tools for grinding glass are vertically mounted, water-lubricated belt sanders or slow-speed lubricated carborundum wheel grinding motors. Grozing is another necessary skill used in making stained glass, and it requires a good deal of practice and patience to master.

WORKING AREA

Working with glass is safe, as long as certain precautions are taken. The first of these is to have an ample amount of room to work. The more space available, the easier it is to have organized, independent work areas for specific functions such as cutting, glazing, and soldering.

CUTTING TABLE

The first thing to do is set up a cutting table, the top of which should be from 30″ to 36″ off the floor. The surface area of the table should be covered with carpet or thick felt. Homosote board is a suitable alternative, and a thick pad of newspapers may be used temporarily. The table surface should be free of any material other than the glass to be cut. Discarded glass chips or pieces should be removed from the tabletop, preferably with a vacuum or a bench brush. Be careful of flying glass particles, and try to brush the pieces into a garbage bag rather than letting them accumulate on the floor.

SAFETY TIPS

When working with glass, always remember to hold the sheet vertically with the hands on top to prevent cuts. When handling glass sheets larger than 20″ × 20″, never hold them flat, as the weight of the glass can easily crack the sheet unexpectedly. When removing a sheet of glass from a worktable, make sure to place it in a vertical position touching the tabletop at about the halfway point of the sheet. Using the midpoint as a fulcrum, raise the top half slowly off the table while easing the bottom down until the sheet is in a horizontal position (Fig. 16). Reverse the procedure to place a large sheet of glass on the table.

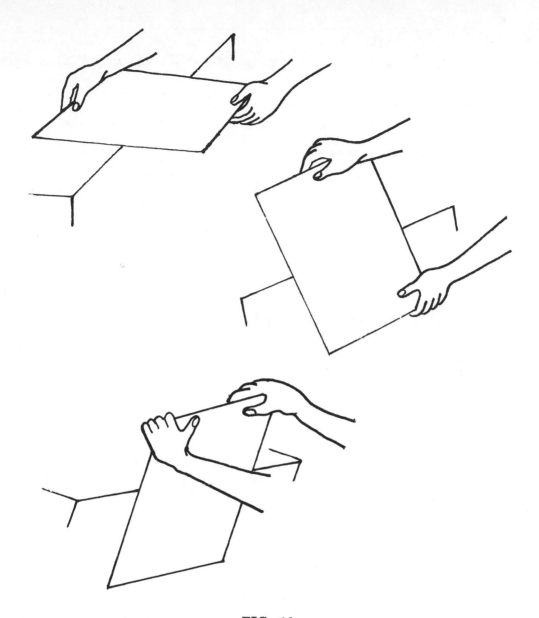

FIG. 16

When lifting or turning a panel or sheet of glass larger than 3 sq. feet, pull the panel or sheet half-way off the edge of the table allowing the panel or sheet to pivot on its center. Slowly lift the top of the panel or sheet away from the table while gently pushing the bottom in toward the table. Now that the sheet is upright, move it or turn it around. At this point, follow the same steps in reverse, as the same procedure applies to any panel or sheet of glass that is to be placed on a flat surface.

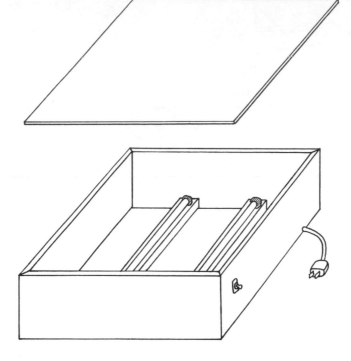

FIG. 17
Light box.

LIGHT BOXES

A light box is a very necessary addition to any workshop, as it enables you to cut glass easily over the pattern and provides a light source for setting up a color scheme. By placing small pieces of glass on the lighted table, you can easily see how the colors interact without having to hold them up to the light. A light box can easily be made (Fig. 17) with the following materials:

2 pieces of wood 1″ × 8″, 40″ long
2 pieces of wood 1″ × 8″, 24″ long
1 piece of wood 24″ × 38½″
2 36″ fluorescent light fixtures and bulbs
1 sheet ¼″ plate glass either frosted or painted white on one side (24″ × 40″)
1 toggle switch

Nail or screw the boards to the plywood bottom, then to each other at the corners, until you have a sturdy box frame. Then insert the fluorescent fixtures, and wire them to the switch. Drill two holes on the side of the box, one for the toggle switch and the other for the electrical cord to slip through. Place a little strip of felt on the top surfaces of the box frame where the glass will sit, plug it in, and you're all set to go.

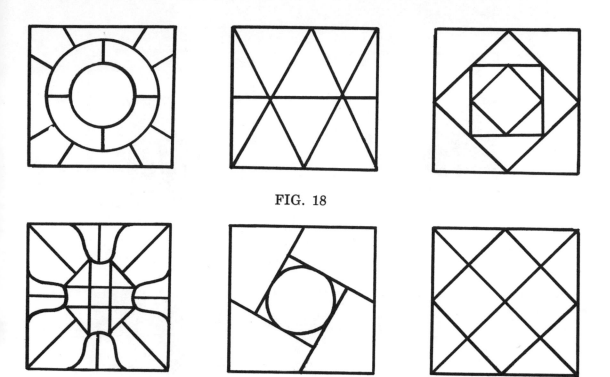

FIG. 18

DESIGN AND PREPARATION

Several factors must be taken into consideration when designing a stained-glass panel, including the limitations of the medium—both physical and structural.

CHOOSING A DESIGN

Although glass may be cut into almost any shape, there are certain unusual shapes which cannot be obtained from a single piece of glass and should therefore be made using two or more sections that require more feasible cuts. As a rule, those just beginning the craft should concentrate on patterns and designs which are based mainly on straight lines and simple curves. The designs in Fig. 18 are examples of easily made basic patterns which can produce larger, more intricate designs if repeated several times. Simple designs like these are best for the beginner and, once mastered, open up a completely new range of design possibilities requiring more complicated cutting. Figure 19 shows some highly intricate cuts, which should be avoided by the novice.

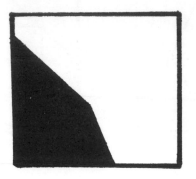

FIG. 19
Impossible cuts.

MAKING A PATTERN

A preliminary sketch must be drawn as you plan your panel. Whether it's simple or complex, sketch your design on medium-weight paper and try to keep it the exact size of your finished piece or within scale. For example, if you want a panel 24″ square, reduce your sketch to a 12″ square piece of paper. Try several sketches with the design until you are satisfied; then study the pieces to be cut. Are they viable? Are some pieces so small that by the time you wrap lead or foil around them they'll be covered up? Start off slowly, and if everything works out in your first few productions, you will then be able to attempt more complex design ideas.

Looking at the pattern, make sure the lead lines will be an integral part of the design and that they are used to achieve a proper balance. If your drawing is scaled down, set up a gridwork

(Fig. 20) on both the sketch and a sheet of medium-weight paper somewhat larger than the size of the piece to be made. This will be the final cartoon. After transferring the sketch to the cartoon, it is necessary to make two full-scale copies of the cartoon—one on medium-weight paper and the other on medium-weight pat-

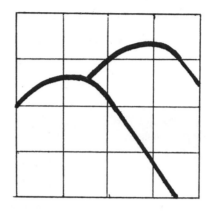

FIG. 20

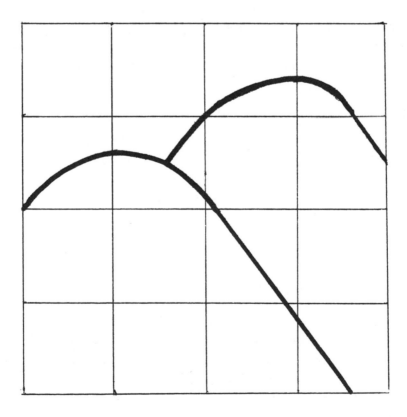

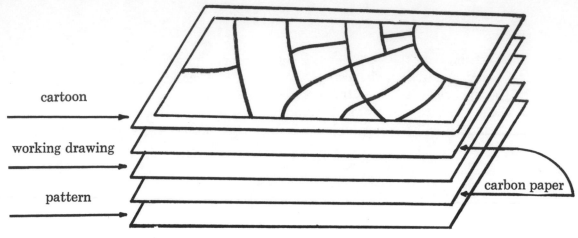

cartoon

working drawing

pattern

carbon paper

FIG. 21

Making copies of a cartoon.

tern paper (oaktag). This is best done by using carbon paper and placing it as shown in Fig. 21.

CHOOSING COLORS

Choosing colors for your design is the most critical part of translating your idea into a pleasing visual image. Basically, all colors are derived from yellow, red, and blue, the primary colors. In the following combinations, these colors produce secondary colors:

Red	Yellow	Blue
+Yellow	+Blue	+Red
Orange	Green	Purple

Then we have the complementary colors, which are opposites:

Yellow—Purple
Red—Green
Blue—Orange

In combination, complementary colors produce various shades of brown.

It is best to lay tracing paper over your pattern to experiment with different color combinations. Using felt-tip pens, crayons, or watercolors, color in all spaces. After doing several drawings, review them and decide which of the color combinations works best. Three basic color schemes can be employed: triadic, using all three primary colors; analogous, using two primary colors; and monochromatic, using only one color in different hues. At this stage, it is best to number and color-code the separate pieces to be cut. Once you have completed the paper work, it is time to cut and trim the pattern paper.

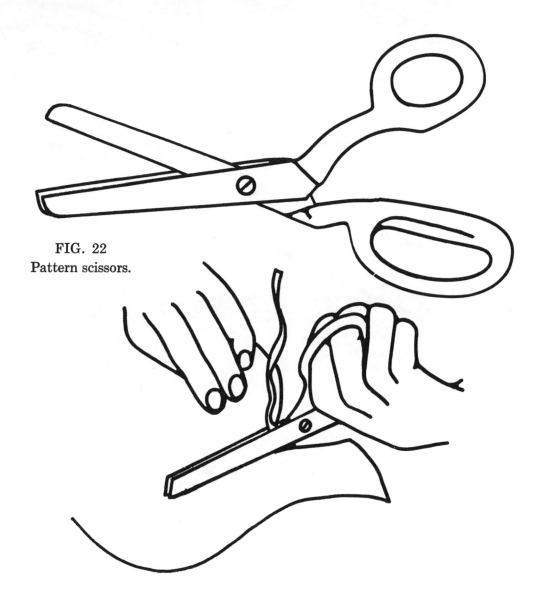

FIG. 22
Pattern scissors.

FIG. 23
Using pattern scissors to cut paper pattern.

CUTTING PATTERNS FOR LEADING

It is best to use pattern scissors (Fig. 22), which are designed to cut out a thin strip of pattern paper equal to and allowing for the heart of the came (Fig. 23). This step cannot be overlooked. If allowance is not made for the lead came, the pattern will be thrown off completely, and the finished panel will be inaccurate.

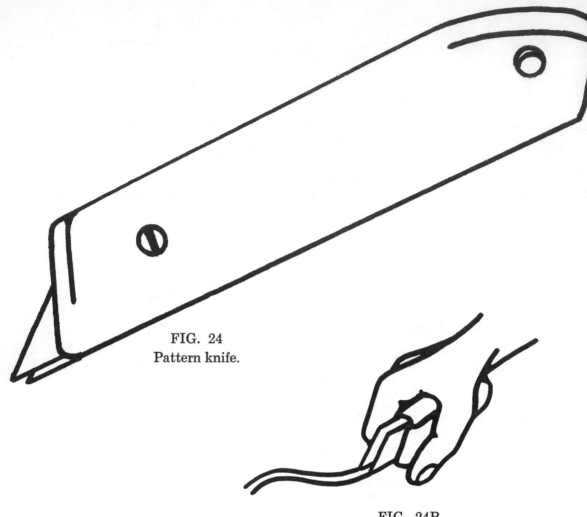

FIG. 24
Pattern knife.

FIG. 24B
Using a pattern knife to cut paper pattern.

CUTTING PATTERNS FOR FOILING

When working with foil, an edge must be allowed for; but since foil is much thinner than lead, a smaller strip should be removed between the pattern pieces. This can best be accomplished with a pattern knife, which is basically a utility knife that has two blades (Figs. 24A, 24B) instead of one and features a shim in the middle to separate the two. A pattern knife can easily be made by unscrewing the two sections of the utility knife, taking two of the blades, placing a thin shim ($\frac{1}{32}''$) between them, and taping them together. Then replace the blades in the knife and tighten the screw.

CUTTING THE GLASS FROM
THE PATTERN

There are two ways of using the pattern for cutting glass. The first is to cut freehand on top of the pattern, a method very popular in France. The procedure is a simple one: The pattern is drawn and two copies made, one for working and the other for layout. The working drawing should have crisp, dark outlines. When cutting the pieces, all cut lines should fall on the inside of the pattern lines to allow for leading and foiling. This method requires very good cutting ability and should be used only after the completion of a few basic projects. When using this method, lighter colors and tints are easily cut right on the pattern, whereas darker colors will require a light source from underneath in order for the pattern to be seen clearly. Another alternative for freehand cutting of dark glass is to cut a paper pattern, lay it on the glass, and using a ponce bag (almost any small piece of fabric filled with whiting will do), lightly dust the pattern, especially around the edges. Then lift the pattern off carefully and you will have a perfect outline of the piece to be cut.

The second method involves laying the pattern on the surface of the glass and holding it down with one hand while using the cutter to trace the pattern onto the glass (Fig. 25). Determine

FIG. 25
Pattern cutting.

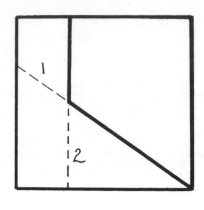

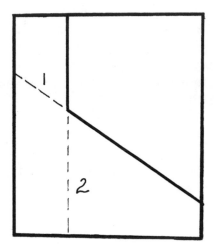

FIG. 26
Eliminating the bisection of an angle by a score line. Fig. A shows the incorrect approach. Line 1 when scored and broken will result in the loss of the sharp corner tip. In fig. B, line 1 *does not* bisect the corner and will therefore result in a clean, even break.

which of the cuts is most difficult, and attempt that cut first. Study the pattern piece and make sure the cuts are made in such a way that they do not intersect the corner of the glass. Any time a cut is made that bisects a point, chances are the tip will break off, so allow a little room between the score line and the corners of the glass (Figs. 26A and 26B).

FIG. 27
Wrapping copper foil around a piece of glass.

TWO BASIC METHODS OF GLAZING

There are two basic methods for glazing stained glass. The most familiar is the lead caming process. A more recent innovation, "the Tiffany technique," utilizes copper foil. This method is basically used for smaller objects. It is also a relatively easy procedure.

COPPER FOIL TECHNIQUE

The copper foil method is also referred to as the Tiffany technique, and was introduced by Louis C. Tiffany around the turn of the century. Copper foil is the preferred method for working with very small individual pieces of glass as well as for three-dimensional work. Foil is adhesive-backed and comes in precut rolls of 36 yards. It is available in a variety of widths, the most popular sizes being $\frac{3}{16}''$, $\frac{7}{32}''$, and $\frac{1}{4}''$. Your choice depends on the thickness of the glass used or the desired width of the solder line. Wider sizes of foil are available in $\frac{5}{16}''$, $\frac{3}{8}''$, $\frac{1}{2}''$, $1''$, $6''$, and $12''$, the last two being used mainly for stencil work or for mirror backing.

Working with copper foil is a relatively easy procedure. The major disadvantages of the technique are the difficulty of cutting the glass pieces exactly to size and of getting the glass edges as smooth as possible. Before you begin, make sure the edges are clean and free of any imperfections. Remove the protective paper along the back of the foil as you work. Place the glass edge in the middle of the copper foil strip and, keeping the foil taut, begin to wrap the foil around the glass. Be careful to keep the glass in the middle of the foil so that the same amount of foil shows on both sides (Fig. 27). Overlap the ends of the foil about $\frac{1}{4}''$ and cut

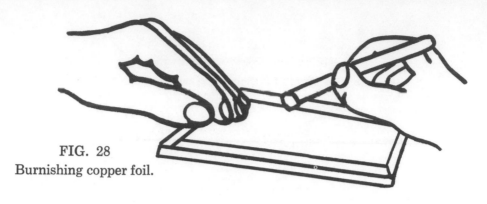

FIG. 28
Burnishing copper foil.

off the excess with scissors or a razor blade. Crimp the foil so it forms a U-shaped channel around the piece, and then press it tightly to the glass with a burnisher (Fig. 28). The piece of glass should be lying flat on your workbench during this process. Discard any foil that becomes twisted and use a fresh piece—it is not worth the time or aggravation to smooth out a worn piece. After wrapping each piece with foil, position it in the design pattern. When all the pieces are fitted into place, your project is ready to be soldered.

Advantages of Copper Foil Technique:

Pliable, easy to manipulate

Inexpensive

Easily soldered

Stronger than lead came because it is soldered on its entire surface, not only at its joints

Lighter in weight than lead came

Will not burn as will lead came

Not as bulky as lead came; produces a more delicate effect

Waterproof; no need to putty

Disadvantages of Copper Foil Technique:

Demands much more accurate cutting

If glass edge is not precise, foil will not hide poor workmanship

Not intended for large pieces of glass

Much harder to repair because it is very difficult to remove broken pieces and replace them with new ones

Requires very fastidious workmanship

More time-consuming than lead came

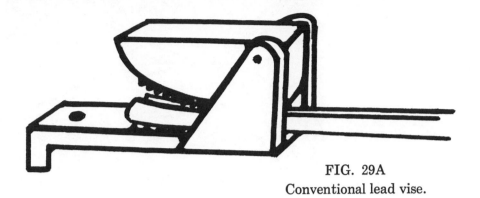

FIG. 29A
Conventional lead vise.

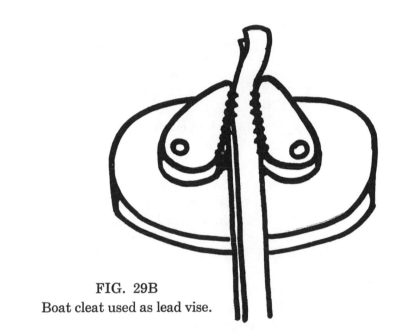

FIG. 29B
Boat cleat used as lead vise.

TRADITIONAL LEAD TECHNIQUE

Lead came should be stretched before actual use to remove kinks and give the lead more body. Then a vise is used (Fig. 29A), preferably a lead vise because of its compactness, reliability, and ease of operation. An alternative would be a boat or yacht cleat (Fig. 29B).

Insert one end of the came approximately 1″ into the vise. Using a pair of serrated pliers, grip the other end of the came securely. At this point, move back until the came is semitaut and position your body carefully. This is one operation that requires a "landing strip," an area directly behind the person, where

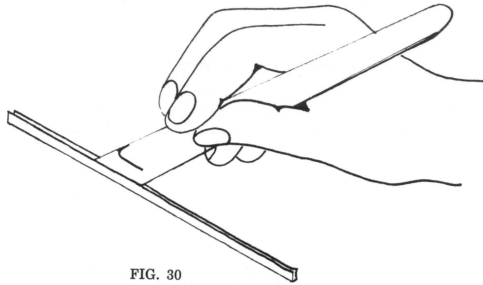

FIG. 30
Using a lathekin to open up lead channel.

he or she can regain balance should the lead slip or split during stretching. If there are any twists in the lead, untwist them by turning the pliers until the channel is straight. This is not a tug of war, so yanking or excessive force are worthless. Gripping the pliers with both hands, give the lead a smooth, uniform pull. The lead will give very easily and will usually stretch about 6″. It is best to stretch the entire length of came at once rather than to try stretching little pieces individually. After stretching the came, lay it flat on a worktable. Using a lathekin, open the channel(s) (Fig. 30), and the lead is now ready to be cut and used.

Leaded glass is the term most widely used in conjunction with stained glass. Basically, the term refers to the method used in assembling small pieces of glass into one unit. Lead came is actually the medium, and the term "came" is derived from Old English meaning "strip." These lead strips generally come in 6′ lengths and are composed of lead and antimony. They are very flexible due to the softness and malleability of the lead, which comes in many different configurations (Fig. 31).

The two most common shapes are H and U, the letters representing a cross-sectional view of the lead. The H-channel is used mainly to unite two pieces of glass together, and the U-channel is best for finishing off a panel and providing a smooth, flat outside edge, which is why it is also referred to as finishing lead.

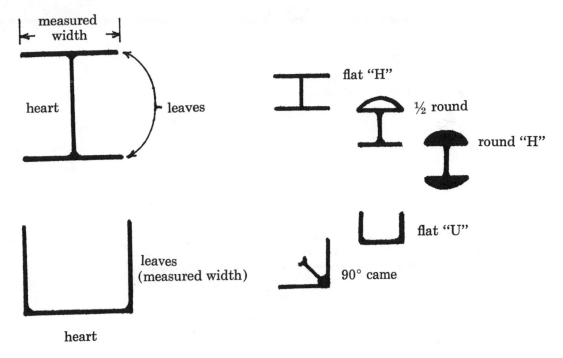

FIG. 31
Cross sectional views and description of lead cames.

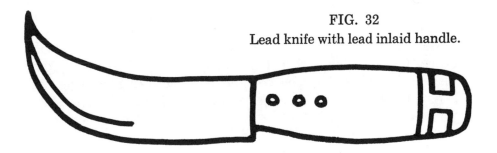

FIG. 32
Lead knife with lead inlaid handle.

Because lead is a soft metal, it is best cut with a very sharp knife called a glazing knife (Fig. 32). The cutting action is much different from that of an ordinary knife, and the cut is made by placing the middle of the blade on the lead channel at the desired point and angle of cut to be made. Then the knife is rocked from side to side with a firm, constant pressure; a clean, smooth cut should result. Once the blade touches the lead, it should not be necessary to lift or move the contact point of the blade from the cut point.

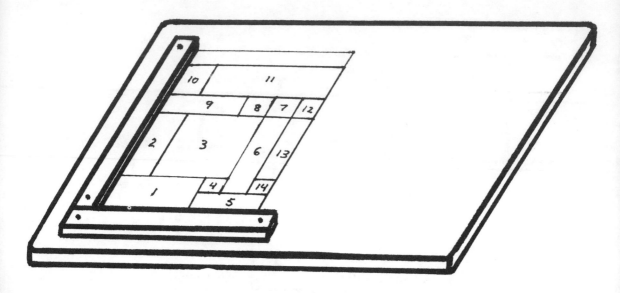

FIG. 33A
How to set up a glazing board with two wood strips
and the working pattern nailed to the work surface.

SETTING UP A GLAZING BOARD

When working with lead or foil, it is best to set up a glazing
board (Fig. 33A). Start with a plywood or homosote work surface larger than the panel to be assembled. Then lay your pattern
on the work surface and cut one strip of $1'' \times 1''$ wood approximately $2''$ longer than the bottom of the working drawing and
a second strip about $2''$ longer than one of the adjacent sides.
Lay the strips at a 90° angle to each other and nail them right
through the outside edge of the working drawing and into the
board. Then cut the lead strips to be used for the outside edge of
the panel and place cut lead pieces of corresponding length
along the wood strips, mitering the corners where they meet (Fig.
33B). In order to glaze all the glass pieces tightly together, start
in one corner and work outward in a concentric progression, keeping the pieces snug against each other by placing glazing nails
along the outside edges of the cut pieces (Figs. 33C and 33D).
There are three basic lead joints (Fig. 34). The mitre and overlap
are generally used around the perimeter of the piece, and the
butt joint is used internally. After all the pieces are in place,
the panel is ready to be soldered.

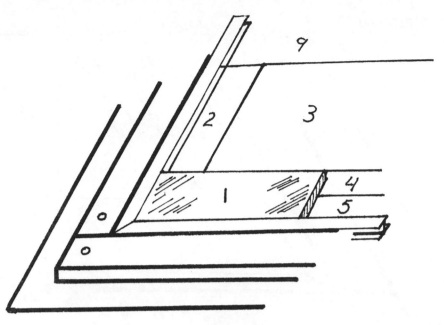

FIG. 33B

Outside lead piece mitred and cut and piece #1 in place.

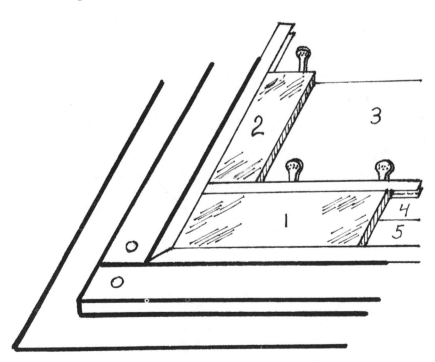

FIG. 33C

Cut pieces #1 and #2 in place along with the lead channel between them.

FIG. 33D

Piece #3 ready to be inserted into the H channel and joined with piece #1 and #2. Note the use of glazing nails to hold the pieces tightly together.

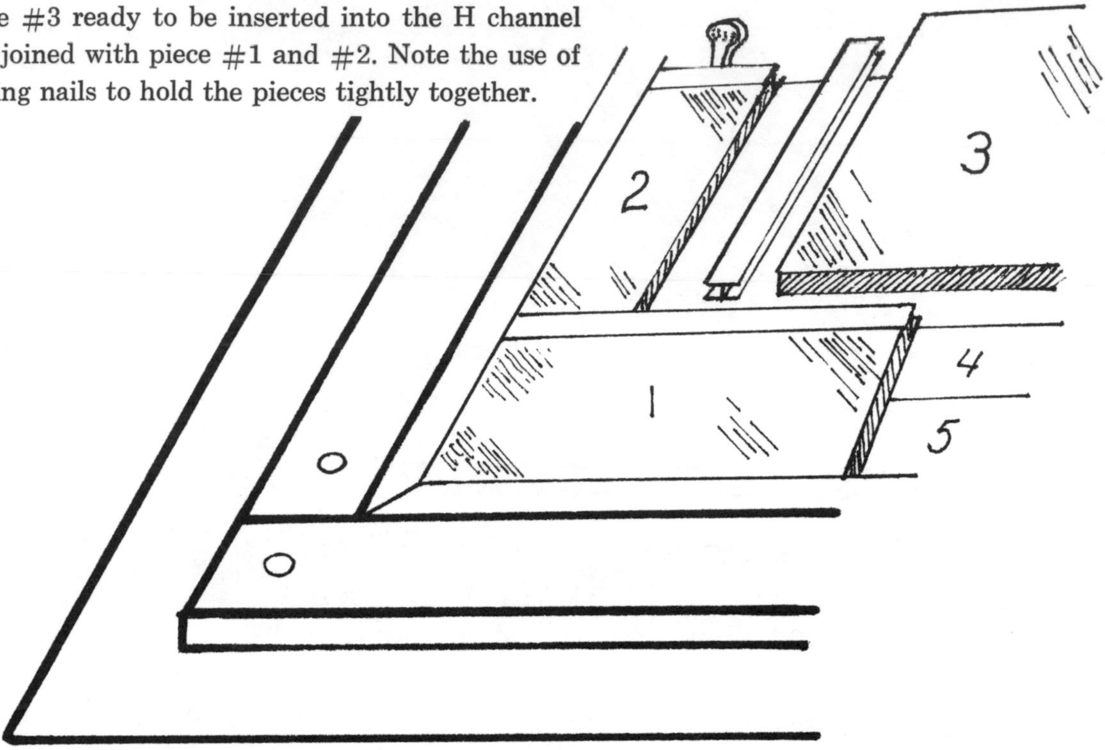

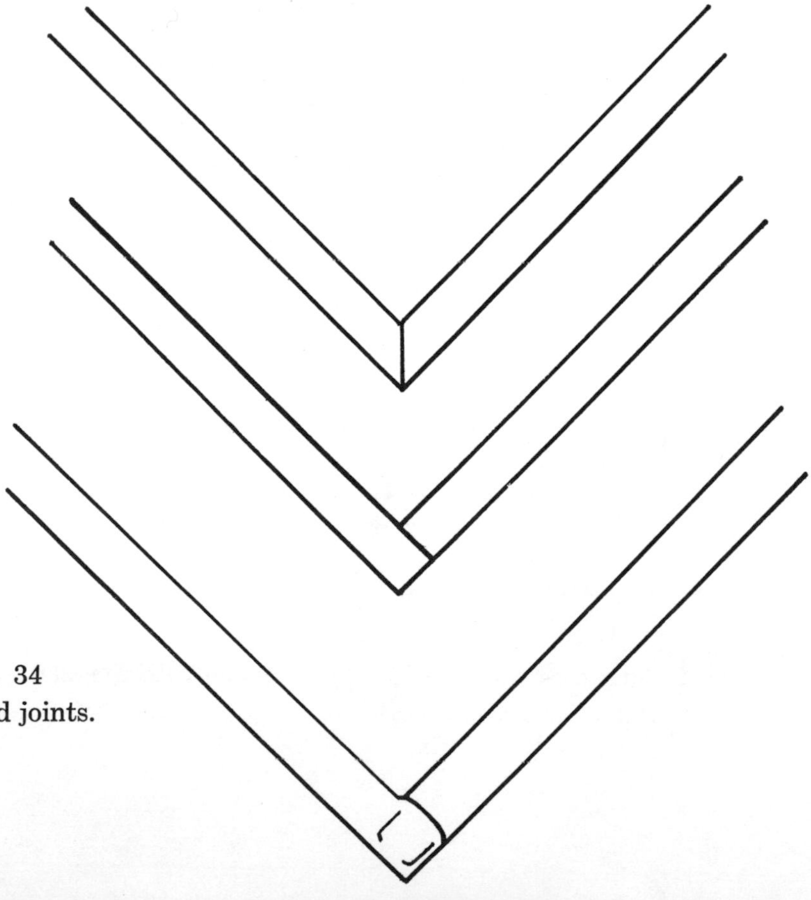

2

3

1

4

5

FIG. 34
Basic lead joints.

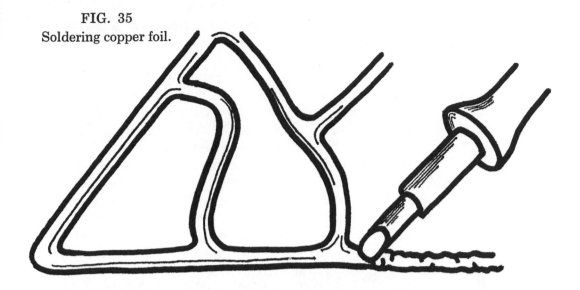

FIG. 35
Soldering copper foil.

SOLDERING

COPPER FOIL

There are three basic steps used when soldering with the copper foil technique: tacking, tinning, and beading. Start by positioning all the pieces exactly in place, using a jig or, if you feel confident enough, just as they lie. Flux all areas to be soldered. This can be done all at once or just on the tack points (strategic places where solder is applied to hold the pieces together as the soldering is completed). Then tin all copper surfaces. If you have applied flux only to the tack points, flux all the top copper surfaces. Tinning means coating the copper with solder, thereby improving the bond between the separate pieces and establishing a base for a good bead. Turn the entire piece over, and repeat the process on the back side. When doing this, place a flat board on top of the piece and hold the entire unit, sandwiching the piece in between the board and the work surface. Flip the panel over, and you're ready to work on the back side.

After you've completed the tinning process, turn the panel over again, and build up your bead (Fig. 35). The bead refers to the solder line produced when working with copper foil. At this stage, more solder is applied until a slightly rounded bead starts to form. After completing this side, repeat the process on the reverse side. Then return to the original front side until a half-rounded, smooth, uniform bead is formed. It is necessary to solder and bead both sides of the panel to assure adequate strength. Remember, the panel should never be turned over without support unless it is smaller than 1' square. Anything larger has sufficient weight to bend and even crack.

On most panels under 4' square, a support is not needed unless the piece is to lie flat without any other surface underneath. The best thing to do in these situations is to solder a ¼" round steel reinforcing bar under the center of the longest side of the panel. The supports should be placed every 2' in both directions. Take advantage of any straight lines in the design that fall in the general vicinity of the needed support, as this simplifies the procedure and adds to the aesthetics of the finished piece. If your panel has no straight lines, the bar may still be used or you can bend a ⅜" flat galvanized steel bar into a form similar to the design lines in the area to be supported. In order to secure the panel to the support bars, solder a piece of ¹⁄₁₆"-diameter copper wire (.064 gauge) about 3" long to the panel on the underside where the support bar will be in contact with the panel. Two 3" lengths of wire should be soldered to the panel where they will contact the bar. The wires should be soldered in the center so that once in place, they can be wrapped snugly around the bar and twisted to eliminate any play or movement.

The same process holds true for upright panels larger than 4' square—there should be support bars approximately every 24" in each direction. After you've figured out where to position the support bars in relation to the panel, the bars may be mounted to a window or door frame. After placing the panel, twist the copper wire ends around the bar and then around each other to bring the panel snugly up against the support bars and lessen the chances of future sagging.

SOLDERING USING LEAD CAME

The most important requirement for lead soldering is a good soldering iron of correct wattage. To help determine your needs, the following wattages are appropriate for these purposes:

25 watts—small, intricate ornamentation, jewelry, boxes

40 watts—same

80 watts—adequate for copper foil work and heavy duty lead work

100 watts—good for most copper foil work where larger amounts are to be coated with solder; can get too hot for lead.

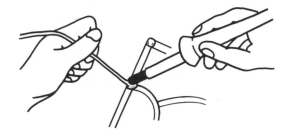

FIG. 36

Soldering a lead joint

A clean surface is also important. Oleic acid, a natural vegetable oil, is the correct flux for lead joint soldering. Apply a light coating of flux to the lead surface at the junctions to be soldered. Holding the roll in hand with the solder wire unwound a few times and pulled straight, place the end of the solder to the tip of the iron directly over the point to be soldered (Fig. 36). There should be just enough solder on the joint to give a clean, uniform appearance to all the lead lines, filling in all excess spaces and gaps.

Now that one side is complete, place the panel flat down and pull it toward the table edge, supporting the bottom. With the top half still on the table, lower the extended portion and use the other end as a lift point until the panel is standing up straight. Turn the panel around so that the unsoldered side is facing you. Then move the panel to the table edge and, still holding it straight up, lower it onto the table, keeping the midpoint flat against the edge. As soon as you reach this point, place one hand on the bottom of the panel and one on the top. Using the table edge as a fulcrum, slowly lift the bottom until half the panel rests flat on the work surface. Then push it gently forward to repeat the soldering process on this side. Once the panel is finished, remember the aforementioned steps when removing it from the table. The lead has no strength when lying flat with no support underneath, and damage can occur to portions or possibly the entire piece. Small panels (under 2′ square) are not hard to handle and may be turned over on the table.

FIG. 37
Basic lamp patterns. The number of sides and the
pattern can be altered to your liking.

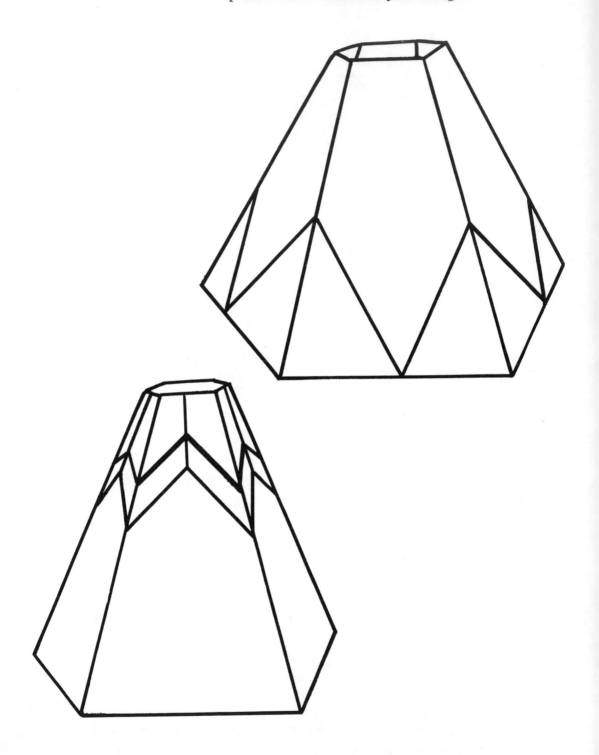

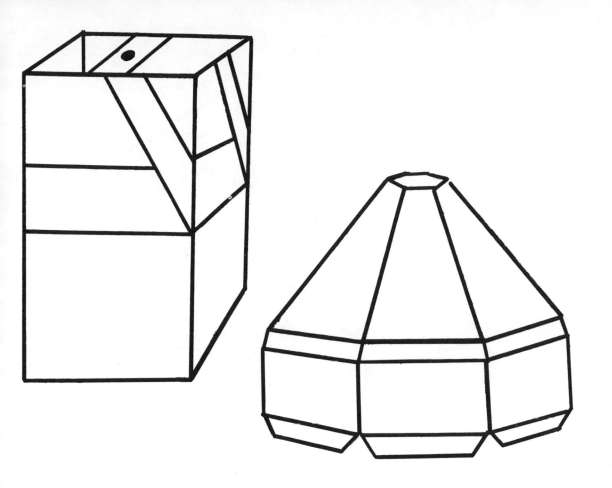

LAMP MAKING

The copper foil method is preferred for lamp making, mainly because of its lighter weight and greater strength.

SHADES

Determine what type and size shade is required, then set up a pattern (Figs. 37A, 37B, 37C, 37D). First consider the number of sides—then cut the pattern so it can be duplicated easily around all sides. Cut all pieces from a heavyweight paper or lightweight cardboard and assemble them with tape or other adhesive. This will give you a three-dimensional look at the lamp's size, shape, and practicality. Foil the glass pieces or cut the lead to the proper lengths. Then lay the pieces flat and, using a minimal amount of solder, tack them together. The flexible crown can now be slowly lifted from the center until the two unconnected sides

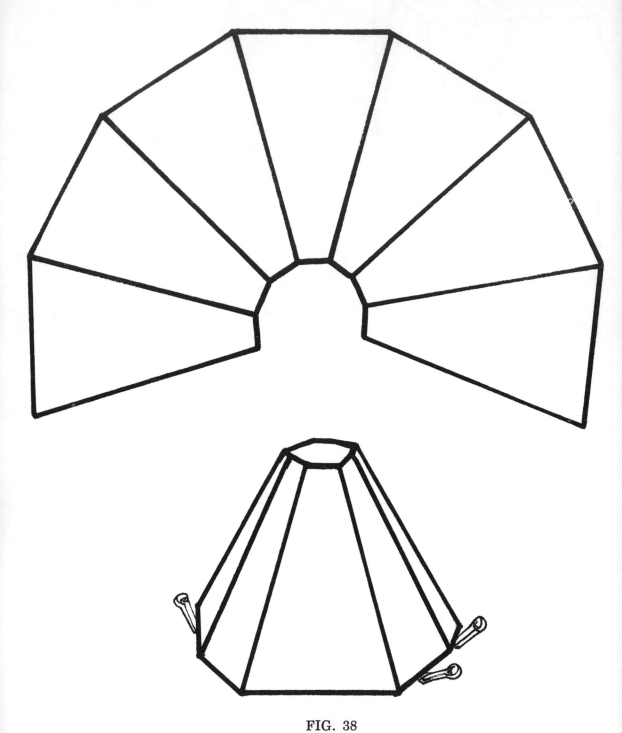

FIG. 38
Fanned out lamp panels. Panels lifted upright and
supported by glazing nails around the base.

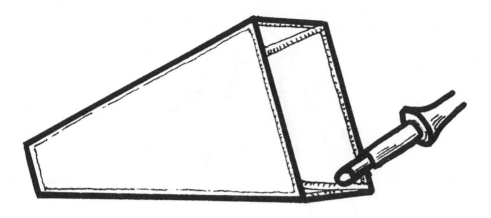

FIG. 39

Laying lamp down in order to get smooth and uniform solder bead.

touch, and they may also be tack-soldered (Fig. 38). Working on homosote board will help because glazing nails can be used around the bottom circumference of the shade to offer needed support and enable one to solder effectively.

To obtain a good bead or solder joint, it is necessary to have the joint or bead line lying flat (Fig. 39) so the solder doesn't run off and is easily controlled. There are a number of ways to do this. If you work on a board (Fig. 40), lift it on one side and shim it with any object that will support it and provide the desired angle. Another method used especially with straight-sided lamps is to lean the lamp on an object that will bring the line to be soldered up to the proper height. Yet another method is to use a wood or cardboard box large enough to fit the lamp into (about 6″ to 8″ high) and fill the box with sand to an inch or so below the top rim. Then position the lamp in the "sandbox" to attain almost any supported position.

FIXTURES

The following items are necessary to make a hanging lamp (Fig. 41):

Ring or loop for hanging

Threaded nipple, ⅛″ I.P.

FIG. 40

Lamp crown joined together and pinned to work
board with glazing nails, making it moveable and
facilitating soldering.

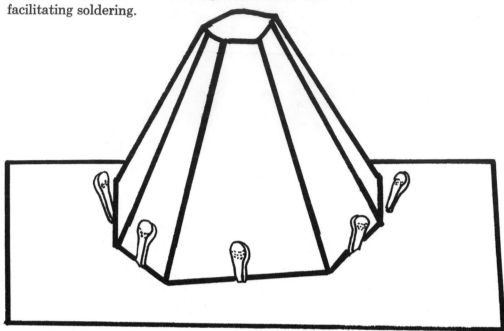

Support bar or vase cap

Threaded nut ⅛″ I.P.

Socket

Electrical wire

Plug

When assembling the lamp supports, remember that the support
bar must be placed so the hole is in the center of the aperture
for balance. If the opening is round, a vase cap is best, but which-
ever you choose, make sure the bar or the cap is a bit larger
than the hole and is soldered onto the inside of the lamp to prevent slipping. On brass caps, it is sometimes preferable to use one
cap for support on the inside of the lamp and another larger cap
on top of the finished lamp. This provides a finished look and
adds extra support.

Choose the right chain to hang your lamp, strong enough and
of a style that reflects the design of the lamp. One of the most
beautiful uses of stained glass is for lamp making, especially when
varieties of opalescent glass are used. The soft, warm glow of a
stained-glass lamp is unsurpassed by any other form of electric
lighting.

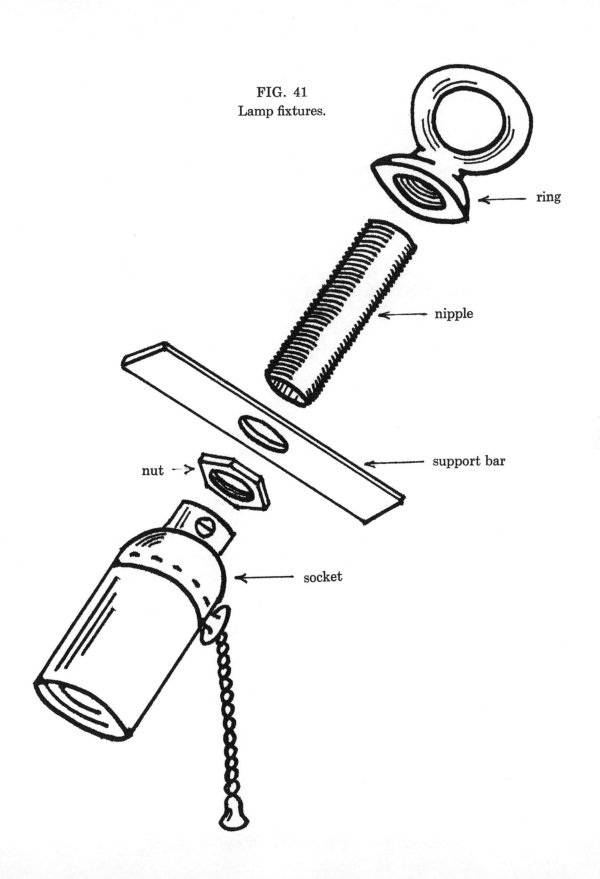

FIG. 41
Lamp fixtures.

ring

nipple

support bar

nut

socket

ETCHING GLASS

The only type of glass used in the etching process is flashed glass, a specially made antique glass having a light base color on one side and a thin layer of another color applied to the other side. The etching process involves removing areas of the flashed side (the thin layer of color distinctly visible when looking at the sides of the glass) to produce a two-color design.

The materials needed are flashed glass, an acid-resist asphaltum, and beeswax or contact paper. You will also need a shallow, acid-proof, plastic tray; hydrofluoric acid; acid-resistant tongs and gloves; and an X-acto knife or similar sharp instrument. If you are not sure of the type of tray to use, call a local chemical-supply house and ask them if the tray you plan to use is capable of resisting hydrofluoric acid.

The resist is applied to all surfaces of the glass to be etched, and the areas to be etched are cut out and removed. Remember that the thinner (flashed) side of the glass is the side to etch, and after the acid has eaten through this thin layer it will reveal the thicker, clearer base color. The contrast between the two is usually very exciting and can be used to achieve either sharp linear contrast or a subtle, diffused interplay of color.

After all areas to be etched have been exposed, the glass must be placed in an acid bath. Ideally, one part acid to five parts water should be used. Remember to always add acid to water when diluting and never water to acid. The bath should be prepared in advance. Use the tongs to lower the glass slowly into the tray. *Caution:* Do not get any acid on your hands or body, as it can cause burns. Wear acid-resistant gloves for protection. Make sure you have proper ventilation when working with the acid. If you're unsure, work outdoors in a place where the prevailing wind is not blowing toward you, or indoors with an exhaust fan in an open window and your acid tray placed close to it. With the glass face-up in the acid, use an acid brush or an old oil-painting brush to remove air bubbles that form on the surface. This will expedite the etching process and remove loose particles that may settle as a result of the acid reaction.

Once the piece of glass looks sufficiently etched, remove it from the acid bath with the tongs. Hold it under lukewarm water for a few minutes, and if it is not etched enough, drop it back into the bath for a short period until the desired results are obtained. You can submerge the glass in acid as many times as necessary. Your final product may be framed by itself or incorporated into a larger panel to add detail and beauty.

GLASS MOSAICS

The mosaic technique allows you to transform pieces of scrap glass into a light-catching design. The glass pieces are usually assembled on a base of clear plate glass and bonded together with clear liquid epoxy. Although use of the transparent glass base is optional, it will capture additional light for your mosaic piece. Grout is available in different colors and is used as a filler for the spaces between the bits of glass. When planning your design, it is important to consider the pattern created by the grout matrix. Geometrical designs lend themselves to this technique and display a rich pattern of color and continuity. For further details, see the Mosaics section of this book.